"Paul Schippel brings to light the deception hidden within false religion. His tenacity and emotion in the pages of this book has lit a fire of revival within my own heart. Its words are aggressive but true and give credence to a God that is the same yesterday, today, and forever."

JOSEPH O'BRIEN
Former Deacon, Pontifical College Josephinum
Columbus, Ohio

"In FROM A PRODIGAL CHURCH TO A PRODIGAL NATION, Author Paul Schippel has presented his very unique and authentic view of the times we are living in and the condition of the modern-day Church. It reveals a deep understanding of the Bible in reference to prophecy and the character of God, who is the same yesterday, today, and forever. Pauls' call to the Church as a 21st century modern day prophetic voice is revealed in the pages.

"This book will motivate the reader into a deeper search for truth and revelation of the mysteries of the Gospel of Jesus Christ."

MINISTER AUDREY KENDRICK
Jacksonville Beach, Florida

FROM A PRODIGAL CHURCH TO A PRODIGAL NATION is essential reading for those who want a deeper understanding into the character of the God we serve. It's a refreshing, honest look at how we have whitewashed God's Word and gotten away from our need to humble ourselves before our Creator...a wake-up call to bring us back into the right relationship He desires to have with us.

BRIAN HAAG
Avid Bible Student
Owner, Windward Construction of South Florida

FROM A PRODIGAL CHURCH TO A PRODIGAL NATION

Paul C. Schippel

Storehouse Media Group, LLC
Jacksonville, Florida

FROM A PRODIGAL CHURCH TO A PRODIGAL NATION

Copyright © 2015 by Paul C. Schippel.

All rights reserved. No part of this publication may be reproduced, distributed, or transmitted in any form or by any means, including photocopying, recording, or other electronic or mechanical methods, without the prior written permission of the publisher, except in the case of brief quotations embodied in critical reviews and certain other noncommercial uses permitted by copyright law. For permission requests, write to the publisher, addressed "Attention: Permissions Coordinator," at the address below.

Storehouse Media Group, LLC
Jacksonville, Florida
www.StorehouseMediaGroup.com
Author@StorehousePublishers.com

Ordering Information:
Quantity sales: Special discounts are available on quantity purchases by corporations, associations, and others. For details, contact the "Special Sales Department" at the email address above.

The views expressed in this work are solely those of the author and do not necessarily reflect the views of the publisher, and the publisher hereby disclaims any responsibility for them.

From a Prodigal Church to a Prodigal Nation / Paul Schippel. — 2nd ed.

ISBN: 978-1-943106-00-4 (paperback)
ISBN: 978-1-943106-01-1 (ebook)

Library of Congress Control Number: 2017957613

Printed in the United States of America

Dedication

This book is dedicated to the glory of the God of Abraham, Isaac, and Jacob the God who never changes.

I want to thank the Lord Jesus Christ who heard my cry in the darkness and saved a wretch like me.

Epigraph

Searching everywhere,
Scanning every nook,
Looking for answers
In the wondrous book.

Knowing what I need,
Craving it at all times;
Needing His presence
In this cruel heart of mine.

Crying for help
On knees stained in blood;
Seeking His face
With tears in a flood.

Begging for mercy,
Begging for grace,
Asking forgiveness
Before losing my place.

He's so close and near,
Not at all hard to find.
I reach out to grab
But slip every time.

On my face I fall,
In desperation I shout.

And in this moment of fear
His love pours out.
Erasing my shame,
Flowing like a river,
Coursing through my veins.

--Karla Gay Schippel

Acknowledgments

Words alone cannot express the heartfelt love I have for one of the greatest treasures God has given me, my beautiful wife Karla who encouraged me and was my most loyal critic in the writing of this book. Her advice and wisdom were moving and refreshing and gave me the courage to go on when times got tough.

I also want to thank my friend Audrey whose prayers and spiritual guidance gave me the boldness to proclaim the truth when others refuse.

And finally, I want to thank Sherrie Clark. Your brutal honesty on this work and your candid critiques helped me become a lot more sensitive to how I express myself in my writing.

And to the Glory of the living God, the God of Israel, who is the same yesterday, today, and forever.

Contents

Introduction xiii

Chapter 1: Christianity: A Religion of Prosperity and Comfort
.... 1
Chapter 2: The American Babylon 15
Chapter 3: Forced Bondage 43
Chapter 4: Apocalyptic Generation 63
Chapter 5: Who to Believe 77
Chapter 6: A Strong Delusion 93
Chapter 7: Trusting God 115
Chapter 8: Unity: The Road to Change 131
Chapter 9: The Power of Grace 149
Chapter 10: A Vision of the Future 163

Author's Note: 175
About the Author: PAUL SCHIPPEL 177

Introduction

What is the purpose of life, and why has God put us here in such a time as this? Why is it so difficult to find happiness, security, and a sense of purpose? Where is this God of the Bible who we have heard of and read about for thousands of generations?

Life is full of everyday challenges that we try to overcome, yet it seems so mundane, so out of our control, and so full of distorted truth.

A church sits on every street corner in America. Our television and radio airwaves and the Internet are full of preachers and teachers, all who claim to have the truth and a more perfect relationship with man's Creator.

In this book, I want to take you on a journey, a quest per say, to the truth of the Word of God. However, you won't hear this truth in the pulpits of America.

From the beginning, I would like to proclaim with no uncertainty that I believe the Bible is the Word of a living God. I declare it is infallible in its original manuscript form. I assert that Jesus Christ is God's Son. I decree that there is no way for man's redemption without faith in the shed blood of the Lamb of God.

I believe in the Holy Spirit and His regenerating power to draw, teach, guide, and comfort everyone who puts faith in the Gospel of Jesus Christ. I believe in the physical return of Jesus Christ to planet Earth during our generation. I also believe He will restore Israel to its former glory and rule and reign from Jerusalem under a theocracy set up through God the Father.

This research of the Word is put into place because some of the things that you'll read in this book will cause you to become angry and ambivalent toward the truth. You'll find truth in the Bible. You'll come across the meat of God's Word, not the milk that you've been suckling on as a Christian.

With that said, let's begin this quest and see if we can discover some answers from the Bible as to the meaning of these truths. Let's explore answers as to why we live in such a time as this, gestating in and awaiting our birth into eternity.

It's your choice whether or not you want to believe the contents of this book. I'm not the author, just the vessel of His chosen mercy.

I admit that I'm also a sinner; a wicked man, a man just like you who was born in sin and shaped in iniquity. I am no one special. I am a mere man who lives under the grace of my Lord and Savior Jesus Christ who chose me before time began to bring forth a word that He has given me.

Judge what you read based on the Bible, not on the religious teaching of man or man's traditions. There's only one truth, and that truth is only found in God's Word. Anything else is lies and fiction born in the heart of hell to deceive and confuse humankind from God's eternal purpose for his or her life.

Jesus said, "I am the way, the truth, and the life. No man comes to God but through me" (John 14:6).

As you read this book, you'll discover scriptures I have referenced and some I just quoted without referencing. I did it this way so that you'd take the time to search them out. As a result, you'd be led to seek out these truths. You'll also find that this is written with very harsh innuendos, like an

Old Testament prophet, so that you can be introduced to the God who never changes.

It's important to understand that God is not a man that He should lie. So why it is we try to whitewash His hardcore truths. I'll never understand why men do this. We have been chosen to be the generation to fulfill God's prophetic plan for the end of age.

Let it not be said of us that we didn't know the time of His visitation (Luke 19:44 ESV) or that we can discern the weather but not the signs of the times (Matthew 16:3 ESV). Please be aware that even though what you read in this book might seem harsh, it's an undeniable truth. If you know and believe the Bible, your only conclusion can be that God is the same yesterday, today, and forever. He is about to show the world this truth in an Old Testament way.

We must prepare ourselves for what we see coming. We have a responsibility to warn and admonish one another and let God work His will through our lives. We have to pay more attention to the facts in scripture for both Old and New Testaments alike. You can't have one without the other, and you can't believe one without the other. It's all truth that never changes.

Hebrews 2:1–3 says, "We must pay the most careful attention, therefore, to what we have heard, so that we do not drift away. For since the message spoken through angels was binding, and every violation and disobedience received its just punishment, how shall we escape if we neglect so great a salvation? ...."

My sincere prayer is that men everywhere would be introduced once again to the God who never changes, to the God who is unchangeable and does not follow the religious precepts of men. I want them to be reintroduced to the God who men served and knew before the Messiah. For over four thousand years before the birth of Christ, men followed God by faith in His name. They served Him because they both loved and feared Him and understood the consequences of disobedience. They witnessed His great power and the right arm of His salvation. They were more than conquerors when the God of Abraham, Isaac, and Jacob was their Lord.

How much more then should we who have received a new covenant through Christ be willing to believe in this God and take a stand for what He has commanded us to do through faith in His name.

As we approach the perilous times ahead, my personal decree is from Joshua 24:15:

> *As for me and my house,*
> *we will serve the God who never changes, and*
> *we will hope in Him.*

CHAPTER 1

Christianity: A Religion of Prosperity and Comfort

One thing that really solidifies that we are in the last days is that Christians have become lazy, weak, materialistic, heady, high-minded, and lovers of pleasures more than lovers of God.

They preach love but gossip about one another continuously. They preach healing, health, wealth, and miracles while they themselves cannot muster up enough faith to see the diseased, sick, and dying in their own churches get healed. Most of their healing services are full of circus acts. I've been in a healing service and personally witnessed supposed men of God taking a person with back problems and having him or her sit in a chair. That "man of God" subsequently pulls on the bottom of that person's shoe so that it appears the leg is growing longer. He then claims that the back problems are fixed.

People fall on the floor acting like they're possessed by what they believe to be the Spirit of God. They run around the church, babble in tongues, laugh uncontrollably, and proclaim it's a move of God. It's a let-us-name-it, claim-it, frame-it, blab-it, and grab-it mentality.

I feel extremely nauseous when I watch these so-called men of God teaching their congregation a cesspool of lies each and every Sunday. The people are so naive and foolish. They just sit there and act like it's normal.

How in the world can we preach the Gospel of Jesus Christ when we look like fools to the world? Why is there such a constant pleading with the congregation for money?

No real miracles are taking place. If you do hear about a miracle of any kind, it usually is nothing that would get the world's attention.

I'm so sick of what I have seen over the last thirty years. I call myself a believer more than I call myself a Christian. What these false teachers have done is pathetic, not to mention the damage created by these wolves in sheep's clothing and these supposed modern-day prophets. I can't mention names because they would sue me so that they could continue to live their lavish lifestyle off the backs of the innocent sheep who don't study God's Word for themselves.

I'm fed up with the lies. The truth must be proclaimed for the Church to hear. Someone has to have the courage to expose these men for what they are. Believe me, if we lived in the time of the Old Testament believers, I can guarantee that Moses would have given the order to put these men to death for the lies and blasphemy they spew from their mouths to deceive the people.

Christianity has become a joke to the world. It has been laughed at and disrespected on television, radio, and in the press on a daily basis. We are mocked and persecuted because of our sins.

Did not our Lord and Savior say, "I have not come to abolish the law but to fulfill it" (Matthew 5:17 ESV)?

We need an Old Testament mentality to rescue the Church from the web of deceit that it has been taught for far too long. We've become a generation of cowards and weak-minded fools who have displayed our dirty laundry in front of the whole world. We then have the audacity to say and believe we're suffering persecution because of our faith in Christ. What a farce.

We're constantly persecuted and made fun of because we have made ourselves look righteous to the world when we're powerless, faithless, and dead.

Have I made you mad yet? I hope so because if hearing the truth makes you mad, then maybe it will give you the faith to believe that the God of the Old Testament is the same yesterday, today, and forever just like His Word declares. Maybe you'll get an Old Testament mentality to do something about it. It seems to me that we've spent so much time in the New Testament that we've forgotten there was an Old Testament God who told the patriarchs of old to condemn all of those who preach worldliness.

Yes, God sent His Son into the world to save and redeem humankind. Jesus shed His blood for the sins of the world and demonstrated God's love and mercy for everyone who would believe.

Yes, He preached that we should love our enemies and forgive those who persecute us for preaching the gospel. That's all true.

However, let's be honest here. Not one verse in the Bible says God changes. Not one verse in the Bible says He needs instruction. Not one verse in the Bible says He makes mistakes. Finally, not one verse in the Bible exists where He tells His people to conform to the world's standard of truth.

I think it's time for people who say they are Christians to start serving the God of Abraham, Isaac, and Jacob, the God of Elijah, Moses, and Joshua, and the God of David, Samson, and Solomon. They need to serve the God who didn't tolerate the injustice of evil men but made laws that were equal to His eternal laws. They must get back to the God who fought for and protected His people and those who stood up for the decrees that He had established.

Does the world know this God, and does modern Christianity proclaim this God? Here is a hypothetical question. What would happen if God ordered Christians to wipe His enemies off the face of the earth so that they would never be remembered anymore?

Could they do it? Would they do it? Would they argue with God and say, "No, Lord, we can't wipe out Your enemies."

New Age thinking Christians think, *Surely, Lord, you're wrong. That was Old Testament; this is New Testament. Remember, Lord, we don't act that way. We're more civilized. We're a new breed of believers. Surely, Lord, you can see that. We let our rulers, those who we elected, dictate our laws. We can't honor your laws, Lord. That's not the way it is anymore.*

Christianity looks down and judges other religions as uncivil and evil while Christians sit around on their behinds letting governments make laws that ban God's laws. What's happening? Has insanity struck the Church? Have we become so pathetic and lazy that we stand still and let elected officials tell us that we can't pray in schools and that we can't post God's laws? Then these same evil political tyrants give men a license to marry other men?

We allow the killing of unborn children in the most sacred place on earth, the womb of women. I wish the purported Church would have the same tenacity to support and defend the Word of God with the same passion and intensity that they display when making sure they get your ten percent every week. (By the way, this was established in the Old Testament.)

Since it's obvious we have forgotten about the God of the Old Testament, let's look back at this God, you know the God who sent Jesus Christ. Let's again consider the God who said, "For I the Lord do not change; …" (Malachi 3:6), and "… with the Lord one day is as a thousand years, and a thousand years as one day" (2 Peter 3:8 ESV).

Just as a personal side note, if you do the math, you'll discover that one hour in God's time is like 41.66666666667 years for man. This is based on a thousand years equaling one day.

Go back and look at God's behavior toward His enemies and sin in the past. We know He is the same yesterday, today, and forever. Hence, everything the prophets of old were told to do under Old Testament law should be taught today so that the people might be saved. If they refuse to repent and intentionally disobey God's law, then God's law should judge them. However, repentance must be preached through Christ so that they can be offered salvation.

Leviticus 20:7–8 says, "Consecrate yourselves and be holy, because I am the Lord your God. Keep my decrees and follow them. I am the Lord who makes you holy."

America understood the validity of forming this

government under biblical principles. It adopted those principles when the founding fathers formed this government. Less than one hundred years ago, adultery, homosexuality, perversion, disobedience to your parents, rebellion, witchcraft, sorcery, theft, and any crime that was committed and considered sin according to biblical standards brought swift and decisive punishment. In some cases when crimes against God's moral code were committed, public executions or long prison sentences were given. Did not the scripture make it perfectly clear that obedience to God's laws would bring a blessing, and disobedience would bring a curse?

Look at the world around you and what you're exposed to everyday from every news outlet. Use that as a barometer to judge for yourself the road and path America has chosen. This kept escalating while the Church of Jesus Christ remains neutral and refuses to take a stand against the moral apathy of government.

If you want to research the scriptures, you'll find that God's laws were put into place so that the people would fear Him, walk in His ways, and keep them holy and pure from the surrounding nations. The Old Testament has a litany of stories of how God commanded His people to put to death all of those who refused to obey His laws. God told his prophets that when they went into the land that He had promised to give them, they should kill all of their enemies, show them no mercy, and wipe them out so that their sin doesn't corrupt them. In effect, they were to destroy them so that they'll have no way to come back and rise up against them in war.

The principles that Moses put into practice is what led Israel to the Promised Land and gave them victory over all of their enemies. God instituted Old Testament precepts for every nation. He required simple obedience from those who would call Him God.

We as Christians look at the Islamic religion and condemn it as wrong. However, did you know that some of these children of Abraham and Hagar are still practicing the laws that God gave Moses?

This country has been so busy trying to tell the world about God's grace and mercy. Yet we have forgotten that the same God who sent Jesus Christ is the God of the Old Testament. No matter how we try to explain the behavior of God in those days, He is the same yesterday, today, and forever. This same God is about to send His Son to bathe the world in blood at His second coming due to the rebellion and wickedness that has filled the hearts of this generation of men.

Israel today is under a constant threat of war because they didn't obey God's command to kill and destroy their enemies and those who practiced the sins mentioned in Leviticus. They're reaping the results of disobedience to God. If God says kill them all and wipe them out, that means to kill them all; no questions asked, no mercy shown.

Why do men in their arrogance think they can do it better than God? Here is a thought-provoking reality. What if we as Christians were as radical about our faith in the God of Abraham, Isaac, and Jacob as the Muslims were about their god?

What if through mercy and love we taught people about God's supreme sacrifice through Jesus Christ but still held onto the harshness of Old Testament law. What if we held Christianity today to the same standards that were given to us by God through Moses? Has God changed?

On the other hand, have people changed the laws of God to excuse their behavior under a banner of religious righteousness? Let me tell you something. Let me tell you a truth and another thought-provoking reality that you can't escape. The Muslims who defend their beliefs, which have gone unchanged, will have more credibility in these last days because they stood on the law that God gave Moses. Shocking, is it not.

America, once a Christian nation, has slipped into an abyss of shame and disgrace. We haven't held onto the core beliefs on which this nation was established less than two hundred fifty years ago. Christianity today is mocked, laughed at, and held in disregard for the foolishness displayed by those who profit by peddling the Word of God.

The American empire will soon cease to exist. The number-one reason for this won't be because of Congress or its presidents but because of the weak-willed faith of Christianity and the lies that have been puked from the pulpits in America.

We cry for revival and want to see the supernatural power of God, but we do nothing but try to build more churches that proclaim a health-and-wealth gospel. I see alleged prophets and men of God on television every week literally weeping for cash. Yet they never shed a tear of repentance for the sins of this nation and its people.

I can't even watch these false teachers anymore without wanting to go "Old Testament" on them. It's a disgusting display of never-ending lies that tell us that in order to walk under the blessings of God we have to follow their specific instructions. Not surprisingly, these directives are based on man's teaching that comes from their own ideas and beliefs instead of the Bible. They intentionally distort God's truth to capitalize on the weak-minded who depend on these teachers for salvation's truth. Then I watch them attack one another's beliefs and convictions in their need to fleece the choicest flock. They are, as the Bible says, wolves in sheep's clothing (Matthew 7:15).

They are forever learning but never come to the knowledge of the truth. They are sons of deception whose only desire is to feed their narcissism and pride, so that they can become part of what they believe is a move of God.

WAKE UP! What is going on today in the churches in America is not a move of God. It's a mockery of truth by evil men who have been blinded by wealth and ego, thinking themselves to be something when they are nothing. Their only desire is to live off the fatness of the church and only preach and teach what the hypocrites want to hear.

The truth is REPENT, FAST, AND SEEK GOD'S FACE. The time is now without delay. Any man who calls himself a minister of the Word of God must repent of this mediocrity that they've allowed in the house of God.

America is a backslidden nation. The Church has encouraged the unfaithfulness of its people by denying the truth laid out in God's Word. It's backsliding into its own shame and nakedness.

A quote that's been credited to George Washington was "We ought to be no less persuaded that the propitious smiles of heaven can never be expected on a nation that disregards the eternal rules of order and right which heaven itself ordained."

I love my country, and it is because of that love that I must tell the truth. I love my God, and it is because of that love that I must testify to that truth. I'm referring to the truth that America is a nation that was established on the fundamental truth of the Word of a living God. But now it's preparing itself for disaster.

We're all responsible, especially me. I'm as guilty as any other man. I've committed sins that would make demons blush, but I found Christ in my time of desperate need. He revealed to me how necessary it was to repent and get back to my first love.

God has made it so simple for us to obey Him. He loves us so very much that He sent His Son into this world to die so that we can be forgiven of our sins and learn how to walk in His ways. He shows us love, mercy, and compassion. What He requires of us is so little for all He gave.

Why do we let religion dictate how we should live for God? We have to walk by the faith we find in His word. It's that simple. We've been commissioned to reach the world for Christ, not look like profit seekers and fools to this world.

Does not His Word say that if any man be in Christ he is a new creation? Didn't He tell us that old things pass away, and all things will become new (2 Corinthians 5:17)?

If we as Christians who live in America don't get back our zeal, we're destined to suffer under the same persecution that is so prevalent in third-world countries. Those believers don't have the excessive luxuries that the believers in America do. Every Sunday we can go into our churches and enjoy beautiful air-conditioned sanctuaries with our nice cushioned seats. We listen to some good contemporary Christian music and then go dine in a nice restaurant after the service.

Meanwhile over in a third-world country, they get up on Sunday to go worship in a tent in the desert, fanning themselves with whatever they can find. They praise God with one instrument, if they're lucky, praying for water and food for the week.

How did this happen? Have we become so self-absorbed that we've forgotten how to serve?

We live like everything is owed to us. If we don't get our way, we blame God and turn our backs on Him. We've become weak-willed, worldly minded, lazy, lukewarm fence straddlers who sit idly by and expect everything with no sacrifice.

I know this is harsh, and again, I'm just as responsible as the next man. The God of heaven is fed up with how we've done nothing but protest over what we have allowed to happen to this country. We protest, and it stops there.

Where are the men of God who will stand up to the unrighteousness of this generation? Where is the Old Testament mentality against sin? Where is the call to come together and take back what we let the thief take from us in the first place?

Many times when I turn on the television to the Christian networks, I hear, "Jesus is coming, and soon we're going to be rescued from God's impending judgment. No worries for us, no suffering, no pain. We're to be gone in the twinkle of an eye."

God a just God. He's a righteous judge.

Can anyone give me an honest answer as to why we have a right to be rescued in the United States? Are we suffering for our faith? Are we dying for our faith? Are we imprisoned for our faith? Are we beaten for our faith?

What gives us the right to be rescued? Why would a righteous and just God rescue us when we have not suffered for our faith at all? We don't even live what we say we believe. Our faith is dead. Calling oneself a Christian simply because of its connotation to integrity is a false narrative. Taking on the status of a Christian does not give us the right to be rescued; it's just a label people now use to support their own agenda.

If anything, it's third-world Christians who are already suffering in great tribulation. Maybe the rapture is meant for them, not the lukewarm. Kind of makes you think of where you are in your walk with God. It is a shaking to your spirit, a reality check of biblical proportions. Who are you in Christ? What does your faith mean to you? Would you forsake everything to live for Him?

Could you give up every worldly possession? Could you forsake everything you love and hold dear and surrender to Him with your whole heart?

The truth is that if we can't, then the Bible says we're not worthy of Him. Therefore, what gives us the right to think we can be rescued from tribulation?

We are the workmanship of God created through Christ. How is it possible we don't recognize the potential of who we can be in Christ by simply surrendering to the will of God? We are a force of power that causes Satan to flee and demons to tremble when we're in a right relationship with God. Satan is powerless because our Commander-in-Chief is the Christ who defeated him on a cross two thousand years ago.

Wake up, saints. Arise from your slumber and take back the ground you have surrendered. Your King is coming, and He will reward those who have given up everything to follow Him. Turn your weakness into strength. Let fear become courage, and let His armor prepare you for battle.

The enemy is in the camp. His name is Deception. His food is religion, and the pleasure he offers is the world.

It's time for believers to sound the battle cry. We will not allow it anymore.

God belongs in our government and in our schools. The cross of Christ and every nativity scene will not be banned but put on display without fear of reprisal from unjust judges and radical court decisions.

Prayer and repentance shall be our national cry. No more making laws that violate God's moral laws. If it means we take up arms to do so, then we do just that. Isn't that what the God of the Old Testament commanded Moses, Joshua, and Samson to do?

We need to make believers warrior-ready. Why are we so afraid? I just can't fathom how people who call themselves Christians can just do nothing. God has not changed, saints. It's time for a reality check.

The same God you refuse to stand for is returning to fight the armies of the earth when they try to destroy Israel. There's not going to be any peace talks or negotiations, no diplomats, ambassadors, senators, or heads of state. He'll gather the birds of the air to eat the flesh of the dead. That is His battle plan. There will be no mercy and only swift justice.

However, you might ask whether Jesus said we're to love our enemies. Of course, He did, but if loving them and warning them doesn't work, then what? Should we let them continue to force us to disobey God's laws? NO!

Where would Christianity have been if it didn't stand up to the tyranny of Catholicism? Where would we have been if Christians didn't stand up against the tyranny of the British? Where would we have been if Christians didn't stand up to the tyranny we faced in the civil war?

Do you think that men of God just stood there and tried to pray away the enemy? They took up arms and reclaimed their freedoms with God's blessing. To me, this is a no-brainier.

If God is for us, who is against us (Romans 8:31)? No weapon that is formed against you shall prosper; ... (Isaiah 54:17 NASB).

The only problem I see is that we would all have to leave our comfort zone and trust God. Ouch! That's asking too much, right?

Imagine what would happen if every saint of God in the United States went to church one Sunday morning, and the pastor told the congregation, "Go home and grab your guns. We're going to Washington to take back our country."

ABC, CBS, NBC, CNN, and FOX would have camera crews ready and waiting for the outcome. If as few as thirty percent of believers signed up, there would be at least one hundred million Christians. It would only take one day to take back our nation.

We have all of the power but don't have the resolve. We don't want to upset the balance of our temporary lives to try to make a difference for future generations. Unfortunately, we don't have enough faith in God to act. We save our faith for planting seeds of prosperity instead of trying to save a nation that was dedicated to God.

Real Godly faith without works is dead, my friends. Don't you dare say you know Him or have faith in Him if you love this world and the things in this world more than you love Him. Your life is not your own. You were bought with a price by the precious blood of Christ.

Everything you have earned, every possession you have acquired, all of the knowledge you have gained outside of Christ will be forever forgotten. A few things that will have value when death greets you are who your Lord is and whether you lived what you believed.

CHAPTER 2

The American Babylon

Son of man, if a country sins against me by being unfaithful and I stretch out my hand against it to cut off its food supply and send famine upon it and kill its men and their animals, even if these three men—Noah, Daniel and Job—were in it, they could save only themselves by their righteousness, declares the Sovereign Lord (Ezekiel 14:13–14).

Because of the sins of the American Babylon, this country will soon go the way of all world empires that have sinned against the God of heaven. It will fall under divine judgment for the murder of over fifty-five million babies since Roe vs. Wade. Just as righteous Abel's blood cried out from the ground against Cain, the blood of the aborted cries out for justice against the American Babylon.

We've become fatted calves prepared for slaughter. The sin of this nation has almost reached the point of no return, and the stench of its evil has corrupted the whole planet.

From heaven and the very throne of God, America will receive as much torture and grief as the glory and luxury she gave herself. In one hour, she will be consumed by fire, death, mourning, and famine.

The Luciferian pride of America will stand in judgment before a Holy God, who has been long-suffering toward this country. He is a merciful God, but we haven't discerned that the trigger of God's wrath is on the way to being pulled.

America has whored herself to almost every nation on earth. Our excessive luxuries have made us a nation of alcoholics, drug addicts, pornographers, child predators, murderers, homosexuals, pleasure seekers, and lovers of the world and not of God. We have become a nation of violence and greed. If you need proof, just turn your television channel to CNN or FOX and witness the insanity. Every form of wickedness imaginable takes place in this country.

God has already sent a curse on our economy. It will never recover. It's too late.

We're a nation of debt, and this debt is projected to escalate to where we owe almost twenty trillion dollars by 2016. To pay off this debt would require one-hundred percent of every taxpayer's check. It can't be done.

Every state in America is in confusion and fear over the uncertainty of where the money will come from to pay for all of the welfare programs. If there are no jobs, and people can't work, there is no tax revenue.

Our government is broke. Social security can't survive. Medicare can't survive. No government program can survive without tax revenue. If people can't work, then the government will fail to function.

Why is this happening to this once-great nation? It's because we've tried to erase every resemblance of our forefathers' beliefs and its Christian heritage. We've turned God into some kind of genie in a bottle who should rescue us in our time of need.

We've elected judges who have tried and succeeded to blot out any references that we were once a Christian nation. They have effectively removed the posting of Bible verses, nativity scenes, crosses, and references to God from almost every public building. In addition, these same judges have passed laws legalizing same sex marriage, the banning of prayer in schools, and the murdering of innocent babies. You can kill an unborn child in this country, but don't you dare touch a spotted owl, or you'll go to prison.

Here is what the American Babylon can expect if there is not a national repentance from its people and the Church. A righteous and holy God will be forced to pronounce judgment on America for its sins. His justice demands it. These are things He has shown me in the spirit and from what the Bible prophesies must take place:

- ✓ There will be devastation that has been unprecedented in world history.
- ✓ God will change the topography of this nation and bring its pride in its natural beauty to shame and discontent.
- ✓ Earthquakes will soon devastate this country. These earthquakes will take place where they are least expected.
- ✓ Giant sink holes will form in the most unexpected

places. America will be stunned and shocked as hundreds of thousands will be affected.
- ✓ Look for volcanoes to erupt and ash to spread across this nation like smoke from a fire.
- ✓ Hail bigger than basketballs and weighing as much as one hundred pounds will fall from the sky, causing millions of dollars in damages.
- ✓ We can expect hurricanes with winds up to two hundred miles per hour. Science will have no earthly explanation, but these hurricanes will be sent by God as judgment against an unrepentant nation. They'll claim it's the result of climate changes when in reality it's the repercussion of God's righteous judgment.
- ✓ Tornadoes will destroy crops, livestock, and life. Super tornados like those that we have never seen in history will become a plague to the land. God will use these whirlwinds to destroy everything in their path to bring the arrogance of America's pride to the knees of repentance.
- ✓ Billions of dollars in damages will be incurred from all of the natural disasters unleashed upon an unrepentant people, and insurance companies will collapse under the financial stress.
- ✓ God will also use the sun to scorch men with severe heat and send fires throughout the land. Skin cancer will kill millions in America and the nations that have committed adultery with her. This sun's searing will bring drought, famine, and bizarre changes in the weather.
- ✓ God will intervene into the affairs of men, but men will become worse and worse and refuse to repent because of their hatred toward God and the love of this world and its pleasures. Although some will repent and turn to Him,

most will think these events are just normal changes in the earth.
- ✓ Men will drop dead from heart attacks, and many will commit suicide from the fear of what is happening to this once-great nation.
- ✓ Many will become drug addicts in an effort to try to escape from reality.
- ✓ Diseases, airborne viruses, and plagues will also be part of God's judgment against this unrepentant nation.
- ✓ Epidemics of various infectious diseases will kill tens of thousands of people. Many will die without receiving any medical help, and medical supplies will be in short supply.
- ✓ Hospitals will have no more room for the dying. People with no hope of recovering will be euthanized on the spot. The loss of life will be staggering.
- ✓ The dead will fill the morgues in unprecedented numbers in every state.
- ✓ America will see unrest around the world and try to assist only to have these nations turn on her, and they'll do so because of God's judgment.
- ✓ There will be looting, civil unrest, rioting, and public execution.
- ✓ God will send terrorist like ants throughout this country. At the writing of this book, we have interfered with Libya, Syria, Egypt, Iraq, Afghanistan, and Iran, all radical Islamic countries. Even if peace comes, these inhabitants will not forget. America is now in three Islamic countries, killing their people while trying to police and govern under the auspice of righteousness and democracy.
- ✓ Americans need to get prepared because Islamic

fundamentalism is gaining strength throughout the United States, Europe, France, and all of the Middle East. Their way to strength is paved with elections and violence. Their number-one goal is to kill Jews, Christians, and Americans. Do not be deceived in believing that these radical Muslims are just going to sit back and take continuous buffeting from whom they believe is the great Satan. They will strike back when it is least expected.

I am telling you now that Al Qaeda and Hamas have agents in this country. They are ready, willing, and able to give their lives to kill and murder Americans. God has revealed this to His people. We'll feel the pain of terrorism in every city in America at some point in the future.

Some of the reasons why these Muslim extremists, ISIS, Al Qaeda, and Hamas hate Americans so much and call us the great Satan are because:

1) Our support of Israel;
2) Our interference in their countries;
3) Our imposition of democratic government;
4) Our imposition of our views; and
5) Our imposition of immorality.

Muslims have followed their core beliefs for thousands of years and won't change for the American way of life. They view America as a cancer that must be destroyed because America is a nation of homosexuals, pornographers, pleasure seekers, adulterers, thieves, liars, and warmongers who don't really care about them as an independent people. They'll kill in the name of Allah without hesitation. Americans had better prepare to reap within its borders what it has sown in these Muslim countries.

Throughout history, God has used foreign armies to bring His people to repentance. He'll do the same in America for the sake of His Holy Name and for the sake of His people.

Americans don't need to feel threatened solely by communism anymore. A greater threat to our way of life and the whole world now exists: Islamic fundamentalism.

I believe when it's all said and done, they'll have made Hitler look like a choirboy. Get ready, America, because it's coming to our shores. The only thing that can save us is to return to the faith of our forefathers and repent before a Holy God.

Over the years, I have heard many preachers say to their congregations that if God does not judge America, He'll have to resurrect Sodom and Gomorrah and apologize. If they only knew how prophetic those words were… Very soon, God will judge this nation for its idolatry and its shaking of its fist in the face of a Holy God.

It's time for God's people to prepare for what is coming. You must not procrastinate or sit passively in compromise. Start storing up food and water for at least a six-month supply. Make a first-aid kit. Think of self-defense and survival.

Get a couple of bicycles, as many as your family needs. Gas will be in short supply. Start gathering batteries, candles, waterproof matches, hand-cranked flashlights, and hand-cranked radios. Solar-powered generators will be needed.

Find a place of refuge or become one for friends and family. I'll speak more on this in detail in Chapter Four.

Prepare to live like Americans lived two hundred years ago. Just think of what you would need to survive if there were no electricity, running water, gas, grocery stores, restaurants, or hospitals.

It's coming, and if you're not prepared, you won't survive. Start seeking the wisdom that God gives freely if we repent and acknowledge Him. Don't dare think it won't happen in this country because right now, it's happening to Christians all over this planet. It will come to America.

This once-great nation has turned its back on the God who founded it. Its bowl of judgment is almost full. Repent and repent now and let God's eternal grace give us the courage and strength to live through the perilous days that lie before us. He will be with us through the fire of His judgment and will redeem us for the sake of His Son. Here is the reality that must be said for every believer to hear.

America needs to repent; this is true, but the entity that's responsible for the demise of America is not its government or its people. It's the Church in America that's in need of repentance.

The churches have failed to be a living testimony of the power of a living God, a God who said, "Jesus Christ is the same yesterday today and forever" (Hebrews 13:8 ESV).

He's the same God who said, "Behold, I give to you power to tread on serpents and scorpions, and over all the power of the enemy and nothing shall by any means hurt you" (Luke 10:19 AKJV). He also promised us in Deuteronomy 31:8 (AKJV) that "And the LORD, he it is that does go before you; he will be with you, he will not fail you, neither forsake you: fear not, neither be dismayed."

The Church no longer has the faith to believe in the God of Abraham, Isaac, and Jacob. It has become a place of entertainment, not of repentance. It's evolved into a place of positive thinking, not of faith. It's transformed into a place of prosperity, not of humility.

If we could only get back our vision of righteousness and holiness and return to our first love, then God could and would restore America. Otherwise, the destruction that will surely come from its fall as a Christian nation will occur. Although the Church has backslidden, its core is under the delusional belief that it will never suffer. It thinks it will escape the judgment of God.

The rapture delusion is why the Church thinks it's safe from harm. I have to tell you that at one time, I believed in a pretribulation rapture too. However, as I began to study the Word of God, I began to realize that no scriptural evidence exists to support this view.

If Jesus would have come out and said, "I'll come back and remove you before the tribulation, and you won't have to go through it," then I would believe it.

In Matthew 24:3, the disciples approached Jesus. "… 'Tell us,' they said, 'when will this happen, and what will be the sign of your coming and of the end of the age?'"

Jesus answered them and gave them a list of things to watch for and expect. I want you to notice Jesus' response in Matthew 24:15–16: "So when you see standing in the holy place 'the abomination that causes desolation,' spoken of through the prophet Daniel--let the reader understand--then let those who are in Judea flee to the mountains."

Well since we know Jesus knows scripture, we can deduce that He was well aware of the fact that the abomination of desolation takes place in the very middle of the tribulation (Daniel 9:27). With that, we can also deduce that even though the disciples were asking Him what the signs of the end of the age would be, Jesus knew they would have died before the end of the age. They wouldn't have to worry about these end-time events.

Therefore, it's obvious that Jesus was talking to end-time believers who would ask the same questions the disciples did when they were alive. They were the first Christians and represented the Church that would soon be born after His death and resurrection.

> *Jesus left the temple and was walking away when his disciples came up to him to call his attention to its buildings. "Do you see all these things?" he asked. "Truly I tell you, not one stone here will be left on another; every one will be thrown down."*
>
> *As Jesus was sitting on the Mount of Olives, the disciples came to him privately. "Tell us," they said, "when will this happen, and what will be the sign of your coming and of the end of the age?"*
>
> *Jesus answered: "Watch out that no one deceives you. For many will come in my name, claiming, 'I am the Messiah,' and will deceive many. You will hear of wars and rumors of wars, but see to it that you are not alarmed. Such things must happen, but the end is still to come. Nation will rise against nation, and kingdom against kingdom. There will be famines and earthquakes in various places. All these are the beginning of birth pains.*
>
> *"Then you will be handed over to be persecuted and put to death, and you` will be hated by all nations because of me. At that time many will turn away from the faith and will betray and hate each other, and many*

false prophets will appear and deceive many people. Because of the increase of wickedness, the love of most will grow cold, but the one who stands firm to the end will be saved. And this gospel of the kingdom will be preached in the whole world as a testimony to all nations, and then the end will come.

"So when you see standing in the holy place 'the abomination that causes desolation,' spoken of through the prophet Daniel—let the reader understand—then let those who are in Judea flee to the mountains. Let no one on the housetop go down to take anything out of the house. Let no one in the field go back to get their cloak. How dreadful it will be in those days for pregnant women and nursing mothers! Pray that your flight will not take place in winter or on the Sabbath. For then there will be great distress, unequaled from the beginning of the world until now—and never to be equaled again.

"If those days had not been cut short, no one would survive, but for the sake of the elect those days will be shortened. At that time if anyone says to you, 'Look, here is the Messiah!' or, 'There he is!' do not believe it. For false messiahs and false prophets will appear and perform great signs and wonders to deceive, if possible, even the elect. See, I have told you ahead of time" (Matthew 24:1–25).

Jesus said that when you see these things then pay attention because your redemption draws nigh. Now why would Jesus tell us to watch for all the things mentioned in Matthew 24 if we were to be removed or raptured prior to these prophetic events? Christians will be here to witness some if not all of these events, which is why Jesus told his disciples (His Church) to watch for these occurrences.

He said that when YOU SEE these things happening, know it is at the door, and this generation would not pass away until all scripture was fulfilled. This is what Paul taught and believed in 2 Thessalonians 2:

> *Now concerning the coming of our Lord Jesus Christ and our being gathered to him, we ask you brothers, not to be quickly shaken in mind or alarmed, either by a spirit or a spoken word, or a letter seeming to be from us, to the effect that the day of the Lord has come. Let no one deceive you in any way. For that day will not come, unless the rebellion comes first, and the man of lawlessness is revealed, the son of destruction,⁰ who opposes and exalts himself against every so-called god or object of worship, so that he takes his seat in the temple of God, proclaiming himself to be God (2 Thessalonians 2:1–4 ESV).*

Sounds like Daniel 9: 27, which tells us, "And he shall confirm the covenant with many for one week: and in the midst of the week he shall cause the sacrifice and the oblation to cease, and for the overspreading of abominations he shall make *it* desolate, even until the consummation, and that determined shall be poured upon the desolate."

Paul makes it perfectly clear that the day of the Lord's return would come after the revealing of the antichrist and the abomination of desolation. This is what he taught and understood to be true.

Nowhere in any of Paul's letters does he specifically say that the Lord will remove believers prior to the prophecies of

Daniel 9:27. As a matter of fact, both Paul and Jesus clearly state that the antichrist is revealed after the above events and collaborated in the prophecies of Daniel 9:27.

I still don't understand why we have this foolish teaching in the Church. It has created nothing but laziness and slumber for the body of Christ.

If all the Christians down through the generations are called the body of Christ, evidently they'll go through some of the tribulation. We have to quit teaching this escapist mentality and start telling the truth to the Church. Does not the scripture teach that in the last days God would send a strong delusion and that they would believe a lie?

When Jesus prayed to the Father in John 17:15, He said, "I pray not that thou shouldest take them out of the world, but that thou shouldest keep them from the evil."

All of Jesus' prayers were meant for all of the generations of believers, not just for the disciples. Today in the body of Christ, unfortunately the majority opinion rules. The men who teach this rapture theory do so because they want to stay in good standings with their peers and in the flow of the mainstream.

In God's wrath, He judged the world in Noah's day. Were Noah and his family raptured away in the sky?

When God judged the Egyptians for the enslavement of the Jews, were His people raptured? When God judged Sodom and Gomorrah, were Lot and his family raptured? No. They were kept safe here on earth and protected by God. Noah was kept in safety where he witnessed and indirectly experienced God's judgment poured out on the world. The Jews were kept safe in Goshen while the Egyptians were bombarded with plagues. Angels guided Lot to a place of safety while God rained down fire and brimstone all around him.

Christians need to wake up and start believing in facts and not the fiction and lies that are being taught in the churches today. The cold hard fact is that this pretribulation-rapture teaching is a cash cow for those who teach it. They peddle the Word of God for profit and teach a false doctrine of escapism to placate donors, while in the meantime they collect millions to live their lavish lifestyle.

Right now, thousands of Christians are dying for their faith all over the world. If anyone needs a rapture, it's them.

Let's get real here, people. Search the scriptures for yourselves. Quit believing the lies and prepare for what's coming. Would it not behoove you to be prepared to go through the tribulation regardless? If the rapture happens, then you'd be greatly surprised. That would be better than expecting a rapture that might never takes place or takes place later on in the tribulation.

Do you actually believe end-time events will take place the way they are portrayed by these charlatans? Do you want your end-time prophetic understanding to be based on the imagination of some deluded few who are making millions off half-truths at your expense?

Wake up! Repent before a Holy God. Let us get back to the truth of God's Word.

What is the greatest commandment? "... 'Thou shalt love the Lord thy God with all thy heart, and with all thy soul, and with thy mind'" (Matthew 22:37).

Stop believing in partially true statements. Lies have been fed to the body of Christ. "... for Satan himself is transformed into an angel of light" (2 Corinthians 11:14 KJB).

Carnality, complacency, and the love of the world are in the Church. It needs to repent of its sin and seek God's face for America. We're too busy trying to get the splinter out of the world's eye, yet we have a redwood tree sticking out of our own eye.

Look, the undeniable truth is that we don't need to just worry about saving the world; we need to worry about saving ourselves. We don't need more programs, more churches, more giving. We need more Holy Ghost power, not political power.

God is our source and strength, not man. He'll save and redeem us, religion won't. Let us get back to the truth of the Bible and let us take on an Islamic boldness and loyalty about our faith in Christ.

Even though I don't agree with their beliefs, I respect their courage and faith. How many of us would die for what we believe in or go to war against any political power that disrespects our God? American Christians are so busy filling the airwaves with cries for money to fund their next big project. At the same time, though, they condemn and judge the world for not believing in our religious teaching. We're too preoccupied with rambling off the same old tiring religious terms instead of standing up for our faith and answering the tough yet honest questions of those to whom we minister.

WAKE UP! We are in the last days.

If the disciples and the prophets lived today, they would tell you that these are the things that the Word of God said would occur in these last days. I am so angry by the lies and deception that I can hardly contain myself.

I go into some churches in America and see people crying for revival. Instead, they get dog-and-pony shows of supposed Holy Ghost laughter, running around the church thinking they're under the influence of the Spirit of God, babbling in tongues with no interpretation, and they think it's a revival. Please!

We are the chosen generation, saints. It is us. We are the Laodicea Church.

Revelation 3:14–22 tells us,

> *To the angel of the church in Laodicea write: These are the words of the Amen, the faithful and true witness, the ruler of God's creation. I know your deeds, that you are neither cold nor hot. I wish you were either one or the other! So because you are lukewarm--neither cold or hot--I am about to spit you out of my mouth. You say, 'I am rich; I have acquired wealth and do not need a thing.' But you do not realize that you are wretched, pitiful, poor, blind and naked. I counsel you to buy from me gold refined in the fire, so you can become rich; and white cloths to wear, so you can cover your shameful nakedness; and salve to put on your eyes, so you can see. Those whom I love I rebuke and discipline. So be earnest and repent. Here I am! I stand at the door and knock. If anyone hears my voice and opens the door, I will come in and eat with that person, and they with me. To the one who is victorious, I will give the right to sit with me on my throne, just as I was victorious and sat down with my Father on his throne. Whoever has ears, let them hear what the Spirit says to the churches.*

In Revelation 3:18, is it not ironic how Jesus told the Church to buy gold from Him, that which has been refined in the fire? It's similar to the way the Church today is busy selling deceptive prophetic books, holy water, holy oil, holy cloths, deceptive prophetic movies, music, and all sorts of money-collecting gimmicks. This proves to me that we are the Laodicea Church.

People, don't waste your time or money on these religious gimmicks. Jesus is standing outside of the doors of the church, knocking and trying to get inside. He wants to put salve on our eyes to heal us of our intentional blindness. He desires to clothe us from the shame and disgrace of the nakedness we have exposed to the world.

We have been lulled into a false security and complacency. We believe that we're so righteous and holy that God is going to come and rescue us from all of the tribulation because we're so faithful.

China is arresting those on the spot who are trying to establish churches and proclaim faith in Christ. The Chinese consider faith in God as a threat to national security and a form of espionage against its government. They persecute, torture, silence, and murder those who continue to proclaim faith in Christ.

What makes us think we are any better than they are and that it will never happen here? What makes us think we won't suffer the same tribulations?

Go back, friends, and reread what happened to nations that turned their backs on God in the Old Testament. Repent, repent, and repent. That is our only hope.

Get ready because every lie you have been taught and everything you have believed will be shaken to its very core. That wicked one, the antichrist, will be revealed with all power and lying wonders so that if it were possible, the very elect will be deceived.

Now we request you, brethren, with regard to the coming of our Lord Jesus Christ and our gathering together to Him, that you not be quickly shaken from your composure or be disturbed either by a spirit or a message or a letter as if from us, to the effect that the day of the Lord has come. Let no one in any way deceive you, for it will not come unless the apostasy comes first, and the man of lawlessness is revealed, the son of destruction, who opposes and exalts himself above every so-called god or object of worship, so that he takes his seat in the temple of God, displaying himself as being God.

Do you not remember that while I was still with you, I was telling you these things? And you know what restrains him now, so that in his time he will be revealed. For the mystery of lawlessness is already at work; only he who now restrains will do so until he is taken out of the way. Then that lawless one will be revealed whom the Lord will slay with the breath of His mouth and bring to an end by the appearance of His coming; that is, the one whose coming is in accord with the activity of Satan, with all power and signs and false wonders, and with all the deception of wickedness for those who perish, because they did not receive the love of the truth so as to be saved. For this reason God will send upon them a deluding influence so that they will believe what is false, in order that they all may be judged who did not believe the truth, but took pleasure in wickedness.

But we should always give thanks to God for you, brethren beloved by the Lord, because God has chosen you from the beginning for salvation through sanctification by the Spirit and faith in the truth. It was for this He called you through our gospel, that you may gain the glory of our Lord Jesus Christ. So then, brethren, stand firm and hold to the traditions which you were taught, whether by word of mouth or by letter from us.

Now may our Lord Jesus Christ Himself and God our Father, who has loved us and given us eternal comfort and good hope by grace, comfort and strengthen your hearts in every good work and word (2 Thessalonians 2:1–17).

In Matthew 24, Jesus had said "WHEN YOU SEE" for a reason. Can you see the connection in what Jesus said in Matthew 24 and what Paul said in 2 Thessalonians 2:1-7? They both are referring to the abomination of desolation. So get ready because the delusion and lie are alive and well in the Church.

Consider this. Again, in Matthew 24, the disciples asked Jesus, "Lord what would be the sign of your coming and the end of the age?"

To what coming do you think the disciple was referring, the alleged rapture or the second coming? Why would Jesus forget the rapture and say in Matthew 24:15 that "When you see the abomination of desolation …"

If the Church is to be gone in a rapture, then why did He even make reference to it as a pivotal point in His return and the end of the age? Bad news folks, and I'm sorry you've been counting on escaping all of these things, but the facts don't lie. The Church is still here. Let that sink into your heart and mind.

Nowhere in the Bible did Jesus tell His disciples—those who represented the Church—that they would be in heaven while all of this was occurring on Earth. As a matter of fact, He told them in no uncertain terms that when it all began to happen, they needed to flee to the mountains.

Don't look back. Run and get out, for there will be great distress unequaled from the beginning of the world. Nevertheless, and for some reason, the Church is taught that they'll be gone, whisked away, and protected while the world suffers and the antichrist reigns. What a delusional fairy tale created by false teachers and prosperity preachers.

What I find the most intriguing is that the Church teaches and believes these lies from hell and has faith in them. However, it doesn't possess the same faith to believe that God can raise the dead, or heal the blind, or cause the deaf to hear again.

The Church has become full of faithless men who will move heaven and earth to teach such lies. In contrast, they won't stand up to its own government for violating the laws of the God, which they claim to love. It's total insanity for the Church to believe that it will escape the judgment of God on earth when the cause of America's problems is because the Church does nothing.

Let your imagination run wild for a minute. Visualize what would happen if today's Church decided to take responsibility for what has happened in America and repented for its negligence. Think what would happen if the Church called for its congregations to go on a fast and seek the God of heaven.

Imagine what would happen if they consolidated all of their financial resources, shook off all of their worldly desires, and came together as one to fight our out-of-control government and restore America back to its founding principles. Envision the Church deciding to live by the laws of God. Consider what would happen if it exercised its God-given Old Testament authority to take back our nation just like the Muslims have done for their idol-god Allah in their own countries.

What if we called on God on our own behalf like Israel did in Egypt? Do you believe in this God, or is He dead in your opinion? What if instead of letting our government kill the unborn, we seek the God of heaven like Moses did, and we go after these murderers? Do you have the courage to believe in this God and the faith it takes to make a stand for the faith that comes through Christ?

This God said, "For I, the LORD, do not change; ..." (Malachi 3:6 ESV).

Jesus said, "Do not think that I have come to abolish the Law of the Prophets; I have not come to abolish them but to fulfill them" (Matthew 5:17 ESV).

The time for the Church to act is now. We can and must return to biblical truth, or we will pay a heavy price for not adhering to the Word of God.

The timing of this rapture will not happen before the start of the tribulation, unlike what they've been taught and have hoped. The Church will suffer through the wrath of man and the partial reign of the antichrist. You can count on it, friends. This is what Lord spoke to my spirit:

Woe to you who have gained riches off the backs of my sheep and have done nothing to protect the innocent. You have taught my people lies and comfort and have made them feel secure and at ease. Their blood will I require at your hand. The day will come when you will give account for letting a nation die because of your do-nothing attitude. I gave you all power over the enemy, all authority, yet you hide behind a veil of escapism and think you will not be held accountable! Repent and I the Lord God will fight for you. Seek my face and turn from this wickedness, and you will know the power of a living God, and I will once again restore you in my righteousness for My name's sake!

Abraham/Israel/Church/Rapture

The angel of the Lord called to Abraham from heaven a second time and said, "I swear by self, declares the Lord, that because you have done this and not withheld your son, your only son, I will surely bless you and make your descendants as numerous as the stars in the sky and as the sand on the seashore. Your descendants will take possession of the cities of their enemies, and through your offspring all nations on earth will be blessed, because you have obeyed me (Genesis 22:15–18).

Understand, then, that those who have faith are children of Abraham. Scripture foresaw that God would justify the Gentiles by faith, and announced the gospel in advance to Abraham: "All nations will be blessed through you." So those who rely on faith are blessed along with Abraham, the man of faith. ... He redeemed us in order that the blessing given to Abraham might come to the Gentiles through Christ Jesus, so that by faith we might receive the promise of the Spirit (Galatians 3:7–9, 14).

I don't think the Church, or Christians in general, fully understands the responsibility that God has given us in our relationship with Israel and our faith in Christ. Every believer who by faith accepts the gospel of Christ and the promise that God gave Abraham has now become Jews, grafted in through faith in Christ.

The Jews who rejected Christ did so for our benefit and out of God's mercy. Their transgression brought the riches of His mercy to the whole world. They fulfilled the plan that God laid out before time began so that the whole world might be saved through their rejection of Jesus Christ.

Soon, that will end. God once again will turn to the people through whom Christ came, and He will restore the fortunes He promised Abraham.

Romans 11:25–26 tells us, "I do not want you to be ignorant of this mystery, brothers and sisters, so that you may not be conceited: Israel has experienced a hardening in part until the full number of the Gentiles has come in, and in this way all Israel will be saved. As it is written: …"

If we look at this verse intelligently, it says clearly that a number has been put in place by God. It's a number He predetermined! It's the number of Gentiles who would by faith accept Jesus Christ as their Savior. Through that faith, they would become Jews and receive the same inheritance that God promised Abraham.

This is why Paul told them in Romans 11:25 not to be ignorant of this mystery and not to be conceited. A time has been set when this will end, and God will once again turn the focus of His attention back onto the original branch from which we were grafted.

In addition, what about the mystery that Paul spoke about, the one of which we need to be aware?

> *In reading this, then, you will be able to understand my insight into the mystery of Christ, which was not made known to people in other generations as it now has been revealed by the Spirit to God's holy apostles and prophets. This mystery is that through the gospel the Gentiles are heirs together with Israel, members together of one body, and sharers together in the promise in Christ Jesus* (Ephesians 3:4–6).

Moreover, you might be shocked to learn that God personally revealed when this would take place and when the time of the Gentiles would come to a close in His Word.

> *Then the angel I had seen standing on the sea and on the land raised his right hand to heaven. And he swore by him who lives for ever and ever, who created the heavens and all that is in them, the earth and all that is in it, and the sea and all that is in it, and said, "There will be no more delay! But in the days when the seventh angel is about to sound his trumpet, THE MYSTERY OF GOD SHALL BE ACCOMPLISHED, just as he announced to his servants the prophets* (Revelation 10:5–7).

The sounding of the seventh trumpet or when it's about to sound ends the time of the Gentiles. That doesn't mean Gentiles can't be saved; it means the consummation of God's plan for the Gentile age has come to a close.

A lot of attention in heaven is on the sounding of this last trumpet. If you notice in Revelation 10:6 and all the way to chapter 12, this trumpet blast causes a change within the Kingdom of God.

In Revelation 11, the two witnesses leave heaven and come to earth. They give testimony of the Kingdom of God and the Gospel of Christ. They are empowered with Old Testament authority to witness and prophesy. The timeline given for their period on earth is one thousand two hundred sixty days or forty-two months. Then they'll be killed, and their bodies will lie in the street for three and a half days. No one will touch them but will leave them lying on the ground. Everyone will gloat over and celebrate their defeat.

God intervenes and rescues the witnesses. He raises them to life. In the very hour they're raised and taken back to heaven, a great earthquake will take place, and seven thousand people will be killed. A tenth of the city then collapses, and yet the seventh trumpet still has yet to sound.

After this earthquake and the resurrection of the two witnesses, the seventh trumpet is blown. This last trumpet causes all of heaven to hear "... The kingdom of the world has become the kingdom of our Lord and of his Christ, and he will reign forever and ever" (Revelation 11:15 ESV).

Upon hearing this announced,

> ... the twenty-four elders seated before the throne of God fall on their faces and worship Him saying, "We give thanks to you, Lord God Almighty, the One who is and who was, for you have taken your great power and have begun to reign. The nations raged, but your wrath came, and the time for the dead to be judged, and for

rewarding your servants, the prophets and saints, and those who fear your name, both small and great, and for destroying the destroyers of the earth (Revelation 11:16–18 ESV).

Believer, can you now see it clearly? What happens at the sounding of the last trumpet, the seventh trumpet?

The nations on Earth are angry. Why? Because the time of God's wrath has begun. He has resurrected the two dead prophets. He has removed believers from the earth and transported them to heaven to reward and judge His servants, saints, prophets, and those who reverence His name.

The time of His reign has begun. Wrath will now be poured out onto the nations and those who are left on earth.

This is it, folks. Here is your CATCHING UP.

Prior to God pouring out His wrath on Earth, let's look at what takes place right before and after the sounding of the seventh trumpet:

1) Revelation 10:7 shows the completion of God's mystery spoken of in Ephesians 3:4–6: When the seventh angel is ABOUT to sound, God's mystery is accomplished for the gentiles and Israel.
2) The two witnesses are on Earth for forty-two months, and then they're killed and soon after resurrected and taken to heaven.
3) The trumpet sounds, and voices in heaven proclaim Revelation 11:15 "... 'The kingdom of the world has become the kingdom of our Lord and of his Christ ....'"
4) The twenty-four elders declare that the time of the reign of Christ has begun.

5) The nations are angry because they now perceive God's wrath has come. He will destroy those who have destroyed the earth.
6) Judging the dead has begun. Rewards are giving to servants, prophets, saints, and those who reverence His name both great and small.
7) God opens His temple in heaven and within is seen the Ark of the Covenant.

Who can deny the validity of the chain of events that take place before and after this last trumpet? Sure doesn't sound like a pretribulation rapture to me.

I'm sorry that you have been deceived into believing the lies of these last-days false prophets who have lulled the Church into complacency and mediocrity. Now that the truth has been told, do your best to make a difference. Share the truth of God's Word, and let a holy fire burn within you to warn the lost and the deceived within the body of Christ.

CHAPTER 3

Forced Bondage

I'm somewhat perplexed on how the Church and Christianity in general have become the modern-day Sadducees and Pharisees.

We strain at an ant and swallow a camel. The Church, and people in general, are so quick to judge and condemn those who disagree with their theology and teaching that believers turn into robotic zombies who become slaves to religious doctrines and bylaws. We want to give off an appearance of righteousness and godliness while we steal and rob from the congregation like it's owed to us.

We build large beautiful churches and live in excessive luxuries. We then have the audacity to graze like cattle at every restaurant like privileged patriarchs while a block away the soup kitchen is struggling to feed the poor of the city. We gossip and slander our neighbor for having a glass of wine or a cold beer while we feed on worldly pleasures at the temple of entertainment like gluttonous scavengers.

Why does the Church think they can privately interpret the Word of God and that their interpretation is the final authority? Have they themselves not read, "Have you faith? have it to yourself before God. Happy is he that condemns not himself in that thing which he allows" (Romans 14:22 AKJV). "Blessed is the man that walks not in the counsel of the ungodly, nor stands in the way of sinners, nor sits in the seat of the scornful (Psalm 1:1 AKJV).

I have a total lack of faith in these pillow prophets. They don't want you to know about things which God actually permits under the very law He put in place. Why? Because they are blind leaders teaching a formatted religion to keep you under the thumb of their law. They want to keep you bound in legalism, which makes you dependent upon their leadership. They think their interpretation of God's Word must fit the teachings dictated by their religious organization.

I'm about to shock you with some truths that will cause you to wonder why you even listen to these blind guides. I'll use the Bible to show them to you.

Now if you believe God changes His mind or that He is not the same yesterday, today, and forever, then you won't believe these things I'm about to share. But if you believe He is the same yesterday, today, and forever, then you'll believe me.

Therefore, as a catalyst of controversy, I will choose the topic of polygamy just to prove how dishonest they are about making sure you don't get the truth, the whole truth, and nothing but the truth. For the record, though, they'll try their hardest to convince you that God has changed and that after Christ came, it all changed. Of course, giving your tithes and offerings, the Sabbath, and the Ten Commandments are the exception to the rule. They say these are the only tenets we're still to believe about Old Testament.

Okay, here it is for your consideration, and folks, you don't have to take my word for it. Find it for yourself in the Bible.

I'll start with King David as an example, someone the Bible describes as "a man after God's own heart." David was attributed to writing most of the Book of Psalms. He earned his reputation as a warrior for killing Goliath when he was just a sheepherder in his father's field. Additionally, his weapon of choice in this quick battle was a slingshot and three smooth stones.

In 1 Kings 15:5, God spoke about David and said, "For David had done what was right in the eyes of the Lord and had not failed to keep any of the Lord's commands all the days of his life—except in the case of Uriah the Hittite."

As the Bible story goes, David was handpicked by God to be king over Israel and to bring Israel into the glory that God had prepared for His people. David was a mighty warrior, a talented musician, a disciplined political leader, and a man who walked under the shadow of the goodness of God.

Everywhere he went he was protected by the God who called him. Everything he touched was blessed. He was the patriarch to our Lord Jesus Christ, going back twenty-seven generations. It was through his bloodline that Christ came.

David had a direct line to God whether it was through a prophet or a priest. He walked in God's will, and the prophets always came to him with a word on what God would have him to do.

With that being said, you can guarantee that David knew Leviticus law. He was well-versed in all of the ordinances, laws, and the ten commandants. He was fully aware of what sin was and what sin was not. If he had any questions, the Lord made sure the answer came through the prophets. I guess it's safe to say that David had a wonderful and obedient relationship with the Lord God.

Here is what I find most interesting about David's life. He had already acquired six wives according to 2 Samuel. He had married three of them before he sinned with Bathsheba.

In 2 Samuel 12, the Bible does more than tell this story of moral failure by David and the sin he committed. It clearly defines what adultery is and what it is not. Having more than one wife is clearly not adultery. What defines adultery is lusting after and taking a woman who is already married to another man.

Then when Nathan the prophet came to him about his sin, listen to what David says in 2 Samuel 12:7–9:

> *... This is what the Lord, the God of Israel says: 'I anointed you king over Israel, and I delivered you from the hand of Saul. I <u>gave your master's house to you, and your master's WIVES into your arms.</u> I gave you all Israel and Judah. And if all this had been too little, <u>I would have given you even more.</u> Why did you despise the word of the Lord by doing what is evil in his eyes? You struck down Uriah the Hittite with the sword and took <u>HIS</u> wife to be your own. ...*

It's not quite as interesting when we read in this passage that God gave David all of his wives. Subsequently, God told David that if the number of wives He gave him had not been enough, He would have given him more.

Look folks, unless you're deaf, dumb, and blind, you can clearly see that David's sin was that he had committed adultery by taking another's man's wife. His sin wasn't about having many wives. To make matters worse, he had the man killed in battle to try to cover his sin.

All throughout Old Testament scripture, you'll find that God allowed and approved of man taking more than one wife. Never once in the Bible is it called a sin. In fact, remember David's son Solomon, whom the Bible says was the wisest man who ever lived. He wrote parts of the Book of Proverbs. Solomon had seven hundred wives and three hundred concubines. He was also responsible for building the second temple.

Now if great men of God like Solomon were sinning by taking all of these wives, don't you think the Bible would have mentioned this fact? Of course, it would have. All that these men were doing were following the truths that were put in place by the law and the patriarchs. You can research it for yourself. I encourage you to get into God's Word and seek theses biblical truths. That's what they are, truths that were put into place so that we could have a personal relationship with God.

Here's a list of great men of God who were heroes of faith and who had more than one wife: Abraham, Isaac, Jacob, Boaz, Caleb, Moses, David, Solomon, Esau, Hosea, Gideon, Saul, Rehoboam, and Simeon. This is just a short list of those who understood God's law and made sure to walk before the Lord with purity of heart.

These men understood the Word of God on a personal level because they communicated with God directly through prophets, through oracles, or through priests. Not once did God tell any of them that having more than one wife was a sin.

In the twelfth chapter of the Book of Numbers, you'll find a perfect picture of God's blessing upon Moses because he decided to take another wife, even though his own brother and his brother's wife disagreed. In fact, Miriam paid a price for speaking out against Moses. In essence, she questioned God's sovereignty, and she questioned and judged God's servant and Prophet Moses.

As a side note, I want to make perfectly clear here I am in no way promoting polygamy, because at the present time, it is illegal in this country. Instead, I'm providing a relevant truth dealing with what I see in scripture. Simply put, polygamy is legal in nearly fifty countries around the world. I think that with the approval of same sex marriage in this country, it won be long before polygamy becomes legal in the United States.

As Christians, we are well-aware of the commandment "Thou shall not commit adultery." I am positive that Moses as well and any other patriarch who lived after him understood that commandment. Still, they all had more than one wife. Quite interesting when you really examine the scriptures, wouldn't you say? I can say with certainty that I'm sure I'll be judged harshly for sharing this truth. I'll probably be labeled as a fanatic who's trying to promote fornication. In reality, I'm trying to get God's people to understand that because other cultures practice things we might disagree with doesn't make them wrong. It's God's business that no moral absolute on this topic can be found in scripture. We should let Him do the job of judging what sin is, and we should quit condemning and judging people for living what they believe.

Like I've said, even though it's a catalyst of controversy, I'll broach another topic that will cause our modern-day

Pharisees and Sadducees to cringe in frustration. They'll wince as I share with you a truth that they like to lord over you to keep you in a prison of religious bondage.

> *For John the Baptist came neither eating bread nor drinking wine, and you say, "He has a demon." The Son of Man came eating and drinking, and you say, "Here is a glutton and a drunkard, a friend of tax collectors and sinners." But wisdom is proved right by all her children* (Luke 7:33–35).

I can remember oh so well when I asked the Lord to come into my life. I sobbed uncontrollably at the altar of a little Pentecostal church in Antioch, California.

The pastor had just preached a message about the coming of Christ and how without Jesus as my Savior I would be left behind and be forced to worship the antichrist. He scared the hell right out of me and scared the heaven right into me.

I experienced a happiness and joy that I had never thought possible. I felt a power around me and a love in me that changed me forever. I was only fifteen years old, and I didn't even know that God existed until that day.

Over the next few weeks while growing in my newfound faith, some people within that church began to take notice of my ambition and desire to know God and serve Him.

With that being said, I found myself in the pastor's office one day sitting across from him. He looked intently into my eyes to tell me the rules. I guess he felt it was time for me to conform to the religious standards that were put into place to assure my salvation according to the doctrines and decrees of the religious elite.

Now understand this. I was a baby Christian, and as such, I wanted to please God and change my life. Whatever was needed to secure my salvation, I wanted to do. Therefore, I did all these things willingly.

You could never imagine the shock that overwhelmed me when I was told I would no longer be allowed to wear bracelets or necklaces. I had to have my hair cut above my ears. I could no longer listen to anything but gospel music. I could only read my Bible and school textbooks. I was only allowed to wear certain clothes, and I was required to be in church every time the doors opened. The shocker was that if I did not speak in tongues, then I didn't have the Holy Spirit.

You talk about being confused. I mean, come on. How was I, or anyone for that matter, supposed to live like that?

So this is what I decided to do. I started studying and reading the Bible for me so that I could find out what God requires of those who love Him. And boy did I read! I prayed and read for hours with careful study, asking Him to give me the wisdom, knowledge, and understanding to comprehend His Word.

That was when I discovered that by the grace of God, we have more freedom in Christ than the religious elite want us to know. It was their way to control those who depend on their pastor or preacher for guidance instead of studying the Bible for themselves.

I decided right then and there that the only absolute I would answer to was God's Word and not man's interpretation of what he claims it says for me. I began to live my life by what the Bible said to me. I was in a personal relationship with God. He was my Father, and I was his adopted son through my faith in Christ, grafted in to share some of the same promises He gave to Abraham.

I've seen with my own eyes the hypocrisy and chains that come when men judge others to be guilty for not conforming to their religious standards. These are the same men who would have called Jesus a glutton or a drunkard and used their interpretation of God's Word to do evil. Yes, it also gives us permission to do what our faith allows without facing the scrutiny and judgment of self-righteous men. It keeps faith between God and us.

I like to have a glass of wine, a casual drink, or maybe a beer if I'm in the mood now and again. I can drink any of these beverages with a clear conscience because I know the Bible does not prohibit me from doing so. It does, however, make it perfectly clear that if these things become excessive and begin to control us, then it becomes sin. At that point, we're not to do those things that cause us to sin.

This precept doesn't only apply to drinking, and this is where the problem lies. Those religious elitists want to tell you that drinking is a sin that will get you thrown into hell. Interesting enough, but they have no problem living in the lap of luxury while some members of their own church can't pay their bills or buy food.

They excessively gossip and spread rumors about one another. They love the world and have all of the latest technological toys. They spend more time on the golf course than in their prayer closet while judging you for having a beer with your friends. Their houses are out of order. Their kids rebel and don't listen. They talk about their spouses and hate their enemies. Then they have the nerve to tell you that you can't be an usher because your hair is too long.

I have watched these so-called Christians judge and condemn their own children. They criticize their own flesh and blood because they may have made a mistake in the past that came from a decision with which the parents didn't agree. Therefore, instead of showing grace, love, and mercy like Christ showed them, they rant and rail against their own children. They pronounce the judgment of hell on them.

Come Sunday, they sing "Amazing Grace," the same grace they're unwilling to show to their own children. It's total insanity to expect your children to respect you as a Christian when you treat them with such disdain.

In addition, these same people think they have a hotline to God and are able to interpret what is right in your life according to their standards. Did not our Lord teach us to get the log out of our own eye before we try to remove a splinter from someone else's eye?

If you want to have a drink, my friend, don't let these white-washed vessels make you feel guilty because of the liberty you enjoy in your relationship with the God who called you. You have every right as a blood-bought, born-again believer to enjoy the things that God has put on this planet as long as it doesn't cause you to sin or cause others to sin.

Of course, I'm not referring to moral absolutes. Those must be followed to the letter. However, when it comes to hair, clothing, jewelry, piercings, music, drinks, food, or even those things on which the Bible is silent, use your God conscience to direct your steps. Remember, you'll be held accountable for the choices you make.

The Bible says that you are blessed if you're not condemned in your conscience by the things that you allow, but you alone are responsible. Romans 14:22 states, "So whatever you believe about these things keep it between yourself and God. Blessed is the one who does not condemn himself by what he approves." In other words, the person who does what he knows is right shouldn't feel guilty. So, if any of these things condemns you, or if you have doubts about them, don't do them.

Again, the Bible clearly states which moral absolutes are definitely deemed as sin and are not permitted at all. These are offenses that God will judge, so don't use the freedom you have in Christ as a license to sin. Weigh each matter carefully and honestly, and ask God for wisdom. He'll lead you down the right path.

As we all grow in this womb of eternity, we mature to become what God has planned for us since the beginning of creation. It's a one-on-one relationship.

In His eyes, we're all the same. We all must strive for the same purpose, and that's to become like Him. We're not to set standards for ourselves because of what man or religion teaches but what His Word has spoken to our hearts and spirits.

What was the greatest commandment? Deuteronomy 6:5 tells us, "Love the Lord your God with all your heart and with all your soul and with all your strength."

Each of us, as independent souls, has a God conscience that was instilled within us at birth. We begin this journey called life trapped in a body from which we can't escape until death's judgment calls us. During this journey, whether it's one day or one hundred years, we begin this quest at conception with a desire to learn.

From the time we leave the womb, we start to gain knowledge. We become transformed and changed by the knowledge we gain. We learn to overcome and adapt to the challenges that are put in front of us. For some it might take time, and for others it might be immediate.

The Apostle Paul described it well. Regardless of how long or what we might learn during this brief time in the tent of this body, we learn the most valuable lesson of all. It's a lesson that will last for all eternity for every soul. We learn to love.

Love is the greatest and most wonderful gift that God has given us. It exceeds everything else in all of creation. Without it, nothing would exist, whether visible or invisible. That's why God demands that we love one another the way He loves us.

We're not to sit on a throne of self-righteousness, looking down on others who are weak in faith and judging them because they don't believe what we believe or follow the religion that we follow.

God makes it rain on the just and unjust alike (Matthew 5:45). What makes us think our ways and teaching supersede the love and grace of God? If different faiths teach different things, why do we look down on those organizations for their beliefs with such disdain and have an attitude of hatred toward what their faith allows?

If God's moral laws are not being broken, then how about we let them live what they believe? Why don't we try to stop forcing our self-imposed bondage upon others just because we disagree with them?

We need a revival in this country. It needs to be a revival of love and not of tongue talking, alleged holy laughter, casting demons out of Christians, or watching a foot grow while some preacher taps someone on the head, and they fall down. Does anyone really think this does a lot to enforce the credibility of the message of Christ?

Moreover, while this circus act goes on, these people actually believe they're doing a service to God and their fellow man. These are the same people who tell me that hell is waiting for me because I might have a drink with my family or friends, or because I listen to the wrong music, or because I go to church on Sunday instead of Saturday. How ridiculous does the Christian community look when it has this type of attitude toward other believers, of always judging, never forgiving, and quick to condemn.

The Church's cry is for revival, but they refuse to tear down the barriers of separation that stand between them in order to save a lost and dying world. This is done all under the guise of trying to prove they have the only way.

Religion is the blood that pumps the heartbeat of hell. Lucifer is winning this war. His plan to destroy the Church is complete if we do not turn back to faith in the Word of God.

Look believers, I'm not condoning anything, any beliefs, any religion, or what is practiced within their religion. However, if someone's faith allows them to live the way the Old Testament patriarchs lived, then what gives me the right to judge and condemn them as being wrong? Unless the Bible is specific on what is sin, I have no right to judge. I'm certain about this. It's the foundation that was laid by our Lord Jesus Christ in the brief time He was able to be a missionary to this world.

Just as a foundation has four corners, Jesus laid the foundation of the four principles of heaven through His love, life, death, and resurrection. These truths—grace, mercy, love, and forgiveness—are what every church in America and the world need to shout from the pulpits, not the religious babble that's a stench in the nostrils of a Holy God. With these four principles, we can focus on the lost and dying instead of our religion and our organizations.

I don't know about you, but imagine for a minute how the face of Christianity would change if we focused more on our faith instead of on our religion? I'm talking about the kind of faith that allowed us to pray and witness the deaf hearing and the blind seeing. How about the lame walking, the crippled dancing, the dead being raised, and the possessed being delivered? Would not these things display the power of God in Christianity?

What if God found enough faith in the Church to see His Old Testament attributes on display for the whole world to see? What if just one of the protestant religions claiming to be the voice of God demonstrated Old Testament characteristics? The world is longing to see the supernatural God we speak of and proclaim. Is He dead? On the other hand, is the Church dead? Why is there no faith in believing that the God who formed man from dust is the same yesterday, today, and forever?

Do you realize what would happen if everyone who called themselves a Christian stood up and said, "Enough! We're taking back our country, our government, and our states. No more will we allow the removal of our God from the public arenas of this nation and say nothing while this government uproots and blasphemes the laws of the living God."

What if Christians decided to take up arms to overthrow the tyranny of a nation that spits in the face of Almighty God on a daily basis? What if we decided to be like Moses, Joshua, Saul, King David, Solomon, or any of the other great patriarchs?

We have had enough of government violating the laws of God. I believe with my whole heart and soul that if the churches in America would repent, fast, seek God's face, and have the same loyalty to the Word of God as they did to their religion, we could be on the threshold of a new reformation.

If we just took all of the financial resources of the churches in America and combined them under a new legal movement based on Old Testament faith and actions, we could restore this country back to its Judeo-Christian faith. Sadly though, these same pillow prophets who tell you to plant a seed so that God can bless you don't have the courage or the nerve to stand up for what they preach unless they can prosper from it. So, they'll go on telling you about the God of miracles and power while they themselves do not have the faith to take a stand for the God in whom they want you to believe.

It's time for the saints of God to put an end to the bondages of manmade religion. God wants you to be happy and to enjoy life, not overburden you with a to-do list of religious law.

I like action movies, so if a good action movie comes out, I'm going to the theatre to watch it. This is something that I enjoy. Well, some religious groups teach that it's a sin if you do things like go to the movies. They'll tell you that God's displeased with this worldly pleasure.

Have these religious teachers ever read their Bible? This great Book is so full of action that if Hollywood wanted, they could get some of their greatest storylines from it.

Remember the story of Samson and how "... the Spirit of the Lord rushed upon him..." (Judges 14:19)? Remember how he killed a thousand Philistines with the jawbone of a donkey?

What about Gideon and the real story of the three hundred men? God had said unto him, "... The Lord is with you, mighty warrior" as Gideon killed the enemies of Israel (Judges 6:12).

Let's not forget Joshua who took control of leading the children of Israel into the Promised Land after Moses died. God told Joshua, "... Be strong and courageous. Do not be afraid; do not be discouraged, for the Lord your God will be with you wherever you go" (Joshua 1:9).

With that, he went forth and killed anything that stood in the way of their taking control of the Promised Land. Now that is what I call some hardcore action.

In your relationship with God and based on His Word, you have a responsibility to discern what you allow your eyes to see and to what you expose your heart and mind. Don't use your freedom in Christ to do things that are contrary to your God conscience. Instead, use it as an opportunity to grow in your relationship with Him and to witness to the world, demonstrating how we walk by faith and not by sight.

If you want to find these truths, just open your Bible to Romans 14:1. Paul wrote, "Accept the one whose faith is weak, without quarreling over disputable matters."

Paul goes on to speak about matters that were contentious among believers in that era of time, specifically in regards to eating meat and sacred days of worship. He said because of some disputable matters, believers were beginning to judge and condemn things and practices they didn't have the faith to understand. He then tells them to stop passing judgment on one another and to be sure that they don't put any obstacle or stumbling block in their brother's way.

He says that if anyone regards something as unclean, then it's unclean for that person. Their conscience convicts them.

Also, as I mentioned earlier, if you know something will offend your brother, then don' do it. If you do, you're not acting in love. Therefore, he says, let us make every effort to do what leads to peace and to mutual edification.

His synopsis is found in Romans 14:1–23:

Him that is weak in the faith receive ye, but not to doubtful disputations. For one believeth that he may eat all things: another, who is weak, eateth herbs. Let not him that eateth despise him that eateth not; and let not him which eateth not judge him that eateth: for God hath received him.[4] Who art thou that judgest another man's servant? to his own master he standeth or falleth. Yea, he shall be holden up: for God is able to make him stand.

One man esteemeth one day above another: another esteemeth every day alike. Let every man be fully persuaded in his own mind. He that regardeth the day, regardeth it unto the Lord; and he that regardeth not the day, to the Lord he doth not regard it. He that eateth, eateth to the Lord, for he giveth God thanks; and he that eateth not, to the Lord he eateth not, and giveth God thanks. For none of us liveth to himself, and no man dieth to himself. For whether we live, we live unto the Lord; and whether we die, we die unto the Lord: whether we live therefore, or die, we are the Lord's. For to this end Christ both died, and rose, and revived, that he might be Lord both of the dead and living.

But why dost thou judge thy brother? or why dost thou set at nought thy brother? for we shall all stand before the judgment seat of Christ. For it is written, As I live, saith the Lord, every knee shall bow to me, and every tongue shall confess to God. So then every one of us shall give account of himself to God. Let us not therefore judge one another any more: but judge this rather, that no man put a stumbling block or an occasion to fall in his brother's way.

I know, and am persuaded by the Lord Jesus, that there is nothing unclean of itself: but to him that esteemeth any thing to be unclean, to him it is unclean. But if thy brother be grieved with thy meat, now walkest thou not charitably. Destroy not him with thy meat, for whom Christ died.

Let not then your good be evil spoken of: For the kingdom of God is not meat and drink; but righteousness, and peace, and joy in the Holy Ghost. For he that in these things serveth Christ is acceptable to God, and approved of men. Let us therefore follow after the things which make for peace, and things wherewith one may edify another. For meat destroy not the work of God. All things indeed are pure; but it is evil for that man who eateth with offence. It is good neither to eat flesh, nor to drink wine, nor any thing whereby thy brother stumbleth, or is offended, or is made weak.

Hast thou faith? have it to thyself before God. Happy is he that condemneth not himself in that thing which he alloweth. And he that doubteth is damned if he eat, because he eateth not of faith: for whatsoever is not of faith is sin.

We walk by faith in a personal relationship with God. He expects us to walk in the way that our faith permits us to walk.

Your relationship with God is not determined by our religion, denomination, or the teachings of man. It is determined by your ability to discern His Word for yourselves.

Look at it this way. If you have children, you raise them in a way you feel is best for them. You allow your kids to do certain things that other parents might think are unacceptable. However, just because they don't like it doesn't mean you're going to change the way you raise your own kids, right?

Say your little girl spends the night at a friend's house, and they have a bedtime of nine o'clock. Are you going to call the parents of your daughter's friend and demand she be allowed to stay up until ten? No, of course not. You honor the household rules where she's staying so as not to offend the parent(s).

That's what Paul is saying. We're in a personal relationship with God. Although we might do things differently or believe certain things, we're not to offend our brothers because of our faith. Honor them when you're with them, and when you're alone, do what your faith allows. Do nothing that would offend them while in their presence. Yes, it's that simple, Church. We have the liberty to live what we believe and to walk with God with what our conscience permits. Just always remember, though, that moral absolutes spoken of in scripture must be followed. We must never ever use our liberty or faith as a license to sin.

Remember, Romans 3:20 says that where there is no knowledge of a law, there is no knowledge of a transgression, but where there is a law, there remains a knowledge of sin.

CHAPTER 4

Apocalyptic Generation

You can almost feel the apocalyptic fever that's in the air like the prophets of old did in generations past. But in this generation, we hear it proclaimed on radio, television, and on the Internet on a daily basis. It can also be read in every newspaper and magazine in the world at any given moment. It's a doomsday scenario played out for all of humanity to consider.

Thousands of websites preach that the end of all things is near and that they have the food and survival equipment you can purchase to be prepared for Armageddon. Hollywood has become obsessed with programs and movies that proclaim the demise of man's existence on planet Earth.

Foreign governments have built underground bunkers. They use them to store seeds, important historical records, and artifacts to preserve man's impact upon this planet for future generations because they believe destruction is coming. It could be a man-made nuclear destruction, a possible meteor impact, or even a massive solar flare that would reduce the earth to a chunk of burning coal.

At the advent of the year 2012, and the end of the Mayan calendar, some thought a Planet X would collide with Earth, causing its immediate destruction and the end of all things. Rest assure, friends, this world does not end by anything man will and can do to this planet. It will end when God Almighty decides to create a new heaven and a new earth. Then and only then will this earth cease to be.

We're definitely living in the generation that will see the second coming of Jesus Christ to this earth. With that being said, let me put your mind at ease on a few things. First, whether we live or die as believers, we belong to the Lord. If we see trouble ahead, it's our responsibility as believers to prepare for it and to trust God to bring us through those times. The Bible declares that a wise man sees trouble and prepares for it (Proverbs 22:3). That means that if you want to store up food and water, do so. It doesn't mean not to have faith but that God has given you the common sense to protect the interest of you and your family.

A good example is what God told Joseph to do as a prince in Egypt. He instructed him to protect both Egypt and Abraham, the father of the Jewish nation who became Israel.

In Genesis 41, Pharaoh had a dream that covered the span of two nights. In it, he saw seven sleek and fat cows that were grazing comfortably along the Nile River. At that time, seven thin and ugly cows came along and ate the seven fat cows. In the next dream he used the same descriptive detail, but he saw heads of wheat that were healthy and plump that were eaten by parched and dying wheat.

The dream troubled him so much that he sent for all of the wise men and magicians to interpret it, but no one was able to do so. If you've read the story, you know that the cupbearer recommended Joseph to Pharaoh as one who could interpret the dream. He and Joseph had served in prison together, and Joseph had interpreted dreams for him.

Joseph was still in prison but was called before Pharaoh. The king told him the dreams, and Joseph said, "I can't do it, but God will give Pharaoh the answer he desires" (Genesis 41:16).

Joseph came back the next day and gave Pharaoh the answer to his dreams. In short, he interpreted them to mean seven years of plenty followed by seven years of famine.

Pharaoh immediately promoted Joseph to second-in-command in all of Egypt to prepare for what was ahead. Over the next seven years, Joseph began the preparation for the famine that had been prophesied.

He immediately began to start storing food and supplies to preserve his life and the lives of the people of Egypt. This resulted in saving the nation of Israel and fulfilling God's promises to Abraham. Anyone who knew God and His Word would have been foolish if they didn't prepare for what we can now look back and clearly see was coming to Egypt. Joseph understood the prophetic words, even when others didn't and prepared God's people accordingly.

Today, all anyone has to do is get a daily dose of the news. Every day on these network news channels, we can see the fulfillment of what the prophets, apostles, and Jesus said would take place in the generation of His coming. Each day and at the same time, the whole world can hear and see the wars and rumors of wars. Earthquakes are happening by the hundreds everyday somewhere on this planet. Signs are in the sun, the stars, and the moon.

How did the prophets know we would be able to see these things two thousand years ago? Jesus was well aware of what the last days would look like. He knew that through radio, television channels like CNN, ABC, CBS, and FOX, and the Internet, the world would be able to see the events that He had prophesied. Everyone would be able to experience the reality of these events all simultaneously.

It's time for God's people to prepare for what's coming like Joseph did. What is coming will be the worst time in the history of humanity.

That's why Jesus said, "And except those days are not shortened, no flesh would be saved: ..." (Matthew 24:22).

We can expect deaths to be in the billions before He returns. This is scary stuff, I know, and believe me, I'm just as concerned as anyone else. If we trust in Him, though, and adhere to His Word to prepare for what we see and know is coming, He'll bring us through the storm. Preparation is the operative word here. Put every possible scenario into consideration as you begin your preparations.

You must secure a place of shelter whether above or below ground that can withstand extreme weather conditions and a possible nuclear strike or a chemical attack. Do not believe the lie that you will be raptured away in the clouds. It's not going to happen before it gets real ugly. You also must get an adequate supply of food, water, and medical supplies.

Have enough guns and ammo to protect yourself from the civil unrest that's sure to follow. If you have to fight to protect your family and yourself, waste no time in meting out justice swiftly and decisively. Believe me, if God commanded the Jews to kill and destroy their enemies, don't let your conscience stand in the way of protecting your children and loved ones. These bands of marauders, who will definitely form after the destruction of America, will rape and kill your wives and daughters without hesitation and kill and possibly rape your sons.

They'll confiscate your supplies and weapons so that they can secure their own survival. Now of course, if they come in peace and have something to offer for the security of your family, then by all means let your conscience guide you on how you approach the situation.

In the time we have left to prepare, build alliances with those who have the same faith and mindset so that in numbers, you can protect one another. If possible, form a preparation group amongst your friends and family where everyone pitches in financially to have a place of refuge when the anarchy comes.

Also, make sure you stock enough supplies to barter with if needed. Store up on alcohol, beer, and wine since they're great bartering tools. Extra water, fuels (like charcoal and oil), candles, and cheap canned goods that have at least a two-year shelf life will come in handy.

Whatever you think makes a good bartering instrument, have it stored up to use like money. Just make sure you don't compromise your own supplies.

Believe me, I know this is alarming to read, but let's be honest. This country is sliding down a greased pole of moral and spiritual decline. Very soon, God's judgment will have to fall. I have heard testimonies of Christians all over America having visions of judgment coming to this country. If the religious leaders in the time of Jesus missed His coming, what makes us think they're correct today about the escapism they love to teach and sell?

I say that if God left Noah on the earth when judgment came and protected him, He'll protect us also. Did not God also tell Noah to prepare? Does not the Bible say it will be like the time of Noah in the last days before he returns?

We need to get a new vision in the body of Christ of what the Word of God accurately says and prepare ourselves based on those principles. In the light of what we have seen over the last ten years, if you take some time to look around, you'll see how the face of America and our government has evolved. Colleges and institutions have dramatically changed and leaned so far left that you can't even pray or quote scripture without the ACLU or some other atheist group breathing down your neck and threatening legal action.

Look, God loves His children too much to bring all of these things to a head without warning us. Unfortunately, man is hardheaded and deaf when it comes to a verbal warning, so He sends disasters of biblical proportions to get our attention. These things are a timepiece that are too painful to ignore and are staged by God to prepare us for the end of man's reign on the planet He created. They are what Jesus called labor pains, and like labor pains, they will become more frequent and intense as the day of God's final judgment unfolds.

People are hoarding up everything they can for survival and getting ready for the collapse of the American empire. Not only America, but also every nation is feeling the global impact of God's upcoming judgment.

The ship of American economic strength is sinking in a

sea of debt. The more we try to bail out the water, we only delay the inevitable.

Humanity is crying for security and hoping for government leadership to politicize an avenue of escape, all in the name of change. Is the truth not scary? If the truth is frightening, could it not be that this is exactly what the prophets in the Bible predicted would happen? Does even the most devout Christian comprehend how close we have come to the consummation of God's time clock of end-time events?

The world as we know it is falling apart. Like in the time of Noah, we need to read the signs and prepare for the trouble we see ahead. Even those who do not serve God and have no faith through their natural eyes can read that something apocalyptic is coming to planet Earth. If they being children of this world can sense what is coming, how much more can the servants of the Most-High God discern?

Child of God, this is the final stages of man's reign. It's up to us to be sensitive to the Holy Spirit and to get ready for the return of the King of creation. We need to awaken to a new faith, a new hope, and a new vision of God Almighty.

God has everything under control, and nothing can happen in nature or to nature unless God allows it. Remember that. What He has preplanned will come to pass. As a believer, it is your responsibility to take up your sword and fulfill your God-granted destiny to take back what Satan has robbed from us and to stand on the foundation of the Word of God. By the faith we have in Him, we can look disaster in the eye. We can proclaim that we will stand strong while God demonstrates His power to a world that has rejected His laws and His council and has built governments of opposition against his precepts. We can stand still and see the salvation of our God and His Christ while every material and worldly thing is destroyed around us.

Do not be robbed of your faith because of what you see coming. We, as believers, are being prepared to rule as kings and priests when the theocracy of God is set up at the appointed time.

God has not promised to keep us from trials, suffering, or pain. He has also not promised us continual financial security and tranquility. What He has promised is to never leave us nor forsake us and that He would provide all of our needs according to His riches in glory.

He said we would never have to beg for bread and that His love, mercy, and grace would sustain us. Even though the future looks bleak and evil, we don't have to fear, for He controls the future. Even if we go through all of the tribulation predicted upon this earth, God controls this world and its governments.

Isaiah 40:15, 17 says, "Behold, the nations are as a drop of a bucket, and are counted as the dust of the scales; … All the nations are as nothing before Him, They are regarded by Him as less than nothing …"

So prepare, family of God. He controls everything, and He will perform mighty things in this chosen age. It's the age He chose to send His Son to regain control over all of world governments and to establish His throne of justice and righteousness.

Sound the alarm to your friends and family. Form alliances to secure the safety of your family with Godly men and women. Fight for what you believe in because it's time for us to be of one mind, one heart, and one spirit. It's time for us to have the guts and backbone to be like Samson and destroy those who have tried to destroy us.

Quit hiding behind this turn-the-other-cheek mentality. This is the type of weakness that has caused this country to turn its back on God.

And as the saying goes, "How's that working out for you?"

Final Countdown

The doomsday clock is changed yearly. Scientists predict what they see in the world based on global governments and nuclear technology within these governments. The clock has been fluctuating back and forth because of world events and the human condition.

As I see it, there is no turning back the clock. Even if things get better, the course of human history has been set. The greatest deception of all time is about to break on the horizon.

He who rebelled in heaven and took a third of the angels with him is on the precipice of revealing himself as the awaited Messiah who will usher man into a golden age. This will be his final act of rebellion that will end with the return of Jesus Christ. Moreover, as Jesus said, unless those days are shortened, no flesh would be saved. How might this happen?

Here is one possible scenario that would deceive all of humankind. As we know, Lucifer is the master of deception. I don't think Lucifer, who God called the Morning Star and Son of the Dawn in Isaiah 14, is going to give up his desire to kill the objects of God's love—mankind— without a fight. He's going to try to make a power grab for earth just like he tried to do in heaven.

The best way and most likely scenario are to falsely emulate the second coming of Christ and to deceive the world into believing he has come from another planet. It will be a planet that's hidden from all of our deep-space telescopes and satellites.

He might use a UFO, or he might use some other supernatural means to cause all of humanity to believe he is the Christ of which every religion speaks. On the other hand, he could come as Islam's Mahdi, as the true son of Abraham through Ishmael who was conceived by the concubine Hagar, and he could show up somewhere in the Middle East.

Maybe Mahdi will be at the Temple Mount. Since the Jews are children of Abraham, and they are all brothers anyway, Satan could deceive the Jews into believing he is their Messiah.

When he comes on the scene, he'll become the most powerful leader in the world. His charisma will mesmerize the masses, and his oratory skills will keep them under his subjection. He will probably amass an invincible coalition of nations in the Middle East that will cause the surrounding countries to give him their total allegiance.

He will also focus his efforts on Israel, deceiving them into a false peace and pretending to be their most benevolent protector. He possibly will even permit them to rebuild the third temple next to the Mosque of Omar, Islam's most holy site.

He'll barter a peace plan, one that will last for seven years. This will provide enough time for Muslims and Jews alike to come to a compromise regarding who has a historical right to the land of Israel. Is it the children of Abraham through Sarah or the children of Abraham through Hagar?

The United Nations or New World Order will herald this new-age Messiah as a leader for which the world has been waiting. He'll be the embodiment of Daniel 11:36: "Then the king will do as he pleases, and he will exalt and magnify himself above every god and will speak monstrous things against the God of gods; and he will prosper until the indignation is finished, for that which is decreed will be done."

He will be Lucifer in the flesh. When he comes to power through his deception to the world, he'll demand absolute allegiance and worship. He'll come as a prophet and a messiah, a man of peace, but he'll end up claiming to be God Almighty.

He'll reveal his true identity in the middle of the seven-year peace treaty by going into the newly rebuilt temple in Jerusalem and claim that he is God. Matthew 24, Daniel 9, and 2 Thessalonians all make mention of this man of sin, son of perdition, and man of lawlessness performing this abominable act in the middle of the seven-year treaty.

The scriptures claim that his coming will be in accordance with satanic activity, with all power and lying wonders. Revelation 13 says the whole earth will be astonished by his power and will follow after him. They'll worship Lucifer, who gives this man his power. They'll say, "Who is like this man? Who can make war or stand up against him?"

You say impossible.

Less than a hundred years ago, a man named Adolf Hitler was able to deceive millions into believing everything he was doing was for the greater good of humanity and Germany. His rise to power was a murderous example of what is to come.

This is one possible scenario that I mentioned above, but be assured that when these things take place, they will come according to the prophecies of the Bible. They are coming at an expeditious rate, and there is nothing anyone can do to stop it.

Prophecy teachers and Bible students have been trying for years to identify this last days' antichrist. I believe, however, that unless he comes right out and tells the world who he is, there's no way to know until he walks into the temple and claims to be the messiah.

He'll make Hitler look like a choirboy. This man of lawlessness will far exceed any tyrant in human history. The scripture makes it clear that he will oppose and exalt himself above every alleged object of worship. He will take a seat in the temple of God and claim he is God Almighty, Creator and Lord.

He'll come with a myriad of false signs, powers, and lying wonders. He'll war against anyone who denies his divinity and will force the world to acknowledge his lordship. His mission is to turn all religions and worship toward him and to use man as a weapon against the one true God, Jesus Christ. He'll gather the armies of the world together to try to war against the God who threw him out of heaven for his pride and rebellion.

Man will be used as the instrument of his vengeance. Out of his hatred and jealousy for humanity, the desire of the antichrist's heart is to destroy the objects of God's mercy and love. This will lead to his demise.

His rebellion will be destroyed on the mountains of Israel. He'll be imprisoned in chains for a thousand years.

Jesus Christ will establish his throne on Earth and take full governmental control of this planet. Yes, we're living in exciting yet scary times, but if we trust in the One who redeemed us, we'll be safe in Earth's darkest hour.

If you're reading this book, and you don' know Jesus

Christ, I encourage you that wherever you are, ask Him into your heart and life. Repent and turn away from the things that have caused division between you and God, and make Him Lord. He will come in and save you and set you free from sin's grip.

He loves you more than you could ever dream or imagine. That is why he sent His One and only Son to die for the sins of man. He wanted to restore us back into the relationship we were meant to have with Him before Adam sinned.

Scripture teaches us that "Greater love has no man than this, that a man lay down his life for his friends" (John 15:13). This is why Jesus left heaven to come to earth to live as a man, so that He could lay His life down for us and show us the love and mercy of His Father.

Now that it has been almost two thousand years since He left, right now you have the greatest opportunity known to humanity in any generation to be ready to meet Him as Lord when He returns.

Please make Him your Lord today.

CHAPTER 5

Who to Believe

At the writing of this chapter, we're basically on the eve of one or more of our national or state elections. We can expect the airwaves to be bombarded with boring speeches, debates, and political attack ads by both the democratic and republican parties.

Every time one of these candidates opens his or her mouth, you just know it's going to be another round of the blame game. I believe they all would rather lie even when the truth fits better. It's just that simple.

This was once a great nation full of hope and faith with the core belief that God Almighty was our Divine Guide and Protector. Unfortunately, it has become a kingdom of pharaohs, which has enslaved the American people through taxation, government control, intrusion, forced participation in programs robbed by governmental oversight, tax dollars used to provide foreign aid to our sworn enemies, and loans to foreign governments that never are repaid.

Apparently, America has become a nation of fools. How else would you explain our government borrowing billions of dollars in aid from other nations just so we can loan it to those nations who will never pay us back? We go to war on borrowed money to protect other countries that are our sworn enemies. We forgive their debt. Then we force the American people to pay taxes on a social security system that's already broke because our government keeps taking from the same system they are elected to protect. This is intentional insanity. How about we protect the interest of the American people?

What has happened is that God has sent such a strong delusion. This nation is rebellious, and we have become blind to the obvious. We have a government that's out of control. It's full of special-interest groups that have gone so far left that we won't survive as a nation if the people do not act.

I just sit back sometimes and think to myself, *So, let me get this straight. I have to pay a social security tax so that I can have a retirement income from what I earn. I work my whole life for this opportunity, and I also pay a Medicaid tax so that I can have affordable healthcare benefits when I reach the set age, correct? Yet our democratic elected leaders rob from this system like it's their personal piggy bank so that they can dole it out to those who don't work. They end up robbing Americans from their hard-earned money so that they can appeal to special interest.*

Seems like extortion to me. If you don't pay or refuse to pay, guess who will be knocking at your door? How is it we can bail out all of the mortgage giants who mismanaged their companies and all of the big car manufactures who underanalyzed the market? Why can we provide financial assistance to foreign governments, and yet we can't forgive the debt of the American tax payer who finances the insanity of our elected leaders?

These idiots don't care about America or its people. They're money-loving power-grabbing thieves who want to live in the lap of luxury at our expense. They only care about their personal political agenda and prosperity and not about the future of their own children or grandchildren. They're lovers of pleasures more than lovers of God. We the American people just go about our lives doing nothing about it, paying into a system that enslaves us.

Seven days before his assassination, John F. Kennedy said, "There is a plot in this country to enslave every man, woman, and child. Before I leave this office, I intend to expose this plot."

Politicians create the problems in this country, and then in their arrogant hypocrisy, they campaign against them. It's a political force of stupidity based on the need to please special-interest groups who want to make sure their candidate is elected to a higher office.

In this country we allow one hundred senators, four hundred thirty-five congressional representatives, one president, and nine Supreme Court justices to rule, enslave, and dictate over three-hundred-million-strong American people. These same politicians make laws that violate the will of the people. In their pride, they try to convince you at election time that what they have done to this country is not their fault and start to play the political blame game.

They are systematically and methodically destroying this country and don't care. We have become a nation of self-indulgent, power-seeking tyrants whose only desire is to push its beliefs onto not only its people but to the whole world.

Some states and its people are starting to rebel because of forced immigration laws and healthcare mandates. They see the idiocy of this current administration. They don't understand how a government such as ours can spend trillions of taxpayers' dollars to protect foreign governments from internal unrest. Yet they don't have the common sense to protect its own borders.

Are they beginning to fear and sense the frustration of the American people? Why has the Department of Homeland Security decided to buy up four hundred fifty million rounds of hollow point .40-caliber ammo and one hundred seventy-five million rounds of .223-caliber rifle ammo? Are they getting ready for civil unrest from the three-hundred-million strong?

We've have moved past the point in this country where elections can no longer remove the corruption of the government. We the people need to rise with a new American revolution to restore the Constitution back to its rightful place as the supreme law of the land. We need those who took an oath to defend America to side with its people and fight back against an out-of-control government. We don't need them to stand idly by while we erode in a cesspool of political correctness.

Right now, the domestic enemy we need to fear is not its people or foreign governments but its corrupt politicians. We the people have pledged alliance to this republic, one nation under God, not to a government that's trying its hardest to destroy this republic.

We can't survive if we don't repent and turn back to the God we have forsaken. We will sink, erode, and decay like the great Titanic that was believed to be unsinkable. Our undoing will be an ocean of debt created by our out-of-touch and out-of-control politicians.

Right now, it's game-on in the nation's capital. Every American should be paying close attention to what these political demons are doing to the American way of life in this healthcare showdown. This country has never been more in debt, and it's unlike anything we have ever faced as a nation. We're slowly drifting into an abyss of financial ruin. The only possible remedy is to take back the reigns of control through a new American revolution and set up a new constitutional government under military oversight.

After order has been established through and by the will of the people, each state should be allowed to decide whether they want to be part of a new American Union, again by the will of its people. Its fundamental principles will be based on the Word of God and the constitution that was put in place by America's founders. Scrap the current tax system that only favors the wealthy, and establish a tax system where every American or legal alien has to pay. Maybe establish a ten-percent earned-income tax with a ten-percent national sales tax.

Scrap every government program that inhibits free commerce, and get rid of all government funding to any organization that does not adhere to biblical principles. Apply the same principles that were used to form the constitution.

All government focus will be on the rebuilding and restructuring of the American way of life. Until we get our house in order, no more borrowing and no more lending.

We'll focus on national security and the security of our friends in Israel who we are biblically tied to as brothers.

No more warmongering to push our ideology on nations that have been around for over six thousand years and have survived throughout human history without American interference. We'll concentrate on the same priorities of our forefathers: national interest and the will of all of the American people instead of a small minority of special-interest groups.

The people must and should maintain a national militia controlled by an elected official in each state. They'll keep the government in check so that the rights of the people can be protected and served alongside the military.

This militia should be contained to one-hundred-thousand strong in every state in the union and should be controlled by each individual state. It must take a sworn oath to protect and serve only the people of their state and this union.

National elections should be held for the president of this new union, but each state should elect the head of its militia. We'll only maintain and support government organizations that fall under and follow constitutional law and protocols. At the same time, we'll create a new national militia that falls under the constitutional clause that specifies our rights to a well-armed private army. This militia can keep government in check from violating the biblical principles on which this nation was founded. However, this band of soldiers will be separate from military rule. It will only come into play within the military if the government gets out of control and tries to make laws that violate the will of the people and constitutional law.

In the event of a foreign invasion or terrorist attack, this new militia can also serve alongside the people and the military to protect the states and this new American union. We can dissolve the National Guard, which exists solely to serve the government anyway, and hand it over to the states and its elected officials.

Sound radical enough? If America is to survive, we need a radical change in the hearts and minds of its people and a return to constitutional oversight of our elected officials. We the people have allowed an out-of-control government to elect one president. To this very day, he can't produce a certificate of live birth proving his eligibility to hold office as President in the United States.

According to Susanne Posel Investigative Headline News April 10, 2013, article "Obama's Lawyers Officially Admit Birth Certificate Is Fake" (www.occupycorporatism.com/ obamas-lawyers-officially-admit-birth-certificate-is-fake/), Obama's own lawyer admitted that the image of his birth certificate was a fraud. After a six-month forensic examination, the image was concluded to be a digital fabrication created to endow the president with needed political support and power.

Delusions of political grandeur and a desire to rule as the preeminent master over all of branches of government have in the past produced men like Adolf Hitler. Similar to Lucifer in his pride, former President Obama, in his arrogance, had suggested to the Supreme Court that they did not have the authority to determine the constitutionality of his policies. We had elected a president who denied the requirement to subject himself to the two-hundred-fifty-year-old constitution because it restricts his political power and lust to be king.

Fifty years ago, he would have been arrested as a communist and spy and deported back to Kenya or executed for treason. Instead, he was protected by left-wing extremists who wanted to set up a totalitarian government under the auspice of a new-world order that circumvents our constitution.

Why have we allowed this to happen? Why have the churches, which are to be bastions of light to this planet, not acted upon this political arrogance and its moral corruption in America as well as in the whole world?

This nation was founded by a biblical mandate given to it by its forefathers. We were commanded to be a light to the nations, a shining city on a hill.

Why aren't the churches in every city in America preaching against this apostasy in government? Christians have the moral and political responsibility to overthrow any government that denies the laws of Almighty God and the Constitution of the United States of America.

The Church is to blame for the moral depravity that is now America. We alone will be held responsible for what we have allowed to happen. The Church will not listen, so God in His mercy has raised up people like Glen Beck, Rush Limbaugh, and Mike Huckabee to herald the disaster that awaits the idleness of His people. Thank God for those who still refuse to back down but stand stronger under constitutional mandate, despite the threat of government accountability and takeover. I can't say the same for those who claim to stand under a biblical mandate that God has given us. Unfortunately, it's a sad testimony to the condition of the Church and the direction it has taken in the last fifty years.

We've chosen the direction of positive thinking, escapism, and eat, drink, and be merry. Churches, please wake up. Those of us who choose to do nothing and sit in the pulpit will be held accountable for this country's landslide into tyranny and moral corruption. Don't you know that we have the God of creation on our side?

If you have the faith to believe that God will keep your ministries alive through your consistent request for money every week, then you should use that same faith to believe in the American way of life. This is true even if that means we have to overthrow the current government and start over again. Newsflash: the government fears the people and its churches.

Why do you think there's such a move to disarm the American people? Why do you think they need to control everything we do? Why do they want to throw out any mention of God from every public arena under the guise of separation of church and state? It's because they fear our resolve if we decide to act.

George Washington has been attributed to have said, "A free people ought not only be armed and disciplined, but they should have sufficient arms and ammunition to maintain a status of independence from any who might attempt to abuse them, which would include their own government!"

If the Church, I mean every church in America, stood on the Constitution formed under biblical mandate, we could take back control of the government. Instead, more and more churches are bowing to government regulation and control. This is a direct slap in the face to biblical teaching and to the principles on which this nation was founded. It's all done under the false teaching of a proposed new-age enlightenment that titillates the itching ears of the far left.

Additionally, the few churches that do see the threat of government are doing the right thing and preparing for an apocalyptic event. The Holy Spirit has shown them that dark days lie ahead if there is no repentance.

The Church has the opportunity to be a David against its Goliath, which is now the United States government. It can pick up its three smooth stones of faith, hope, and love and reestablish one nation under God with liberty and justice for all. If we have to take it back by force, then we do so under the same banner of faith on which this nation was founded.

Do you think God just handed back the Jews their country after they left Egypt? Of course not, and if you do, you're dead wrong. Go back and reread the stories of how God commanded His people to take back control of their land and how they were ordered to keep their governments in check. He is the God who is the same yesterday, today, and forever.

The time has come for us to live what we believe and say, "Enough is enough" rather than hide behind this wall that separates church and state. We've embarrassed and humiliated the memory of our forefathers and disgraced and shamed the faith of our Lord.

The Christians in America must stand on the Word of God and take back this nation by faith, prayer, and force. Otherwise we're doomed to go the way of all empires that let governments overthrow God's Word and the will of its people. We're now at this point in history because we're sitting idly by and doing nothing.

Here are some quotes penned by our forefathers that will give us encouragement and strength as we fight against government intrusion and tyranny:

- ❖ "The General hopes and trusts that every officer and man will endeavor so to live and act as becomes a

Christian solider defending the dearest rights and liberties of his country" (George Washington).
- "For I have sworn upon the altar of God eternal hostility against every form of tyranny over the mind of man" (Thomas Jefferson).
- "The general principles on which the fathers achieved independence were the general principles of Christianity. I will avow that I then believed and now believe that those general principles of Christianity are as eternal and immutable as the existence and attributes of God" (John Adams).
- "We have no government armed with power capable of contending with human passions unbridled by morality and religion. ... Our Constitution is designed only for a moral and religious people. It is wholly inadequate to the government of any other" (John Adams).
- "The reason that Christianity is the best friend of government is because it is the only religion that changes the heart" (Thomas Jefferson).
- "Can the liberties of a nation be thought secure when we have removed their only firm basis, a conviction in the minds of the people that these liberties are the gift of God? That they are not to be violated but with his wrath? I tremble for my country when I reflect that God is just; that his justice cannot sleep forever" (Thomas Jefferson).
- "It is no slight testimonial, both to the merit and worth of Christianity, that in all ages since its promulgation the great masses of those who have risen to eminence by their profound wisdom and integrity have recognized and reverenced Jesus of Nazareth as the Son of the living God" (John Quincy Adams).

- "The highest glory of the American Revolution was this: it connected in one indissoluble bond the principles of civil government with the principles of Christianity" (John Quincy Adams).
- "All must admit that the reception of the teachings of Christ results in the purest patriotism, in the most scrupulous fidelity to public trust, and in the best type of citizenship" (Grover Cleveland).
- "The foundations of our society and our government rest so much on the teaching of the Bible that it would be difficult to support them if faith in these teaching would cease to be practically universal in our country" (Calvin Coolidge).
- "Of the many influences that have shaped the United States of America into a distinctive Nation and people, none may be said to be more fundamental and enduring than the Bible" (Ronald Reagan).

These last two quotes are prophetic of what will become of this once-great nation if Christians don't rise up and take back our country. We are responsible. We have allowed America to turn its back on God. We've become heady and high-minded and loved the world and the things in the world more than the God who redeemed us.

The Spirit of the Lord would say, "Your days have been numbered. Judgment begins in the house of God."

- "... but we have forgotten God. We have forgotten the gracious hand which preserved us in peace, and multiplied and enriched and strengthened us; and we have vainly imagined, in the deceitfulness of our hearts, that all these blessings were produced by some superior wisdom and virtue of our own. Intoxicated with unbroken success, we have become too self-sufficient to feel the necessity of redeeming and preserving grace, too proud to pray to the God that made us" (Abraham Lincoln).

- ❖ "The fundamental basis of this nation's law was given to Moses on the Mount. The fundamental basis of our Bill of Rights comes from the teachings which we get from Exodus and St. Matthew, from Isaiah and St. Paul. I don't think we emphasize that enough these days. If we don't have the proper fundamental moral background, we will finally wind up with a totalitarian government which does not believe in the rights of anybody except the state" (Harry Truman).

We have been chosen by God for such a time as this. We will be held accountable at the coming of our Lord and Savior Jesus Christ.

Will you rise and let your voice be heard on what this great nation was founded? Or will you do nothing and keep silent in comfort and at ease believing you'll escape?

We need to rise up like our founding forefathers did before us and fight for ourselves and for the future of our children. I love this country, and even though I have never served in the armed forces, I respect the history of this nation and the men and women who gave their lives to make sure we remained a free people. They were true patriots who risked everything for our freedoms.

We have a responsibility to try to make a difference. How can we call ourselves Americans yet not do anything to stop this takeover of our nation? Our children and children's children depend on us to restore the American way of life that was founded on the principles of God's Word.

In 2 Chronicles 7:14, God promised us that if His people, who were called by His name, would repent and seek His face, He would forgive us and heal our land. What do we have to lose, saints? Remember how God told Jonah, "Go to the great city of Nineveh and preach against it, because its wickedness has come up before me" (Jonah 1:2).

Jonah had already decided in his heart that Nineveh deserved to be destroyed. So, he decided to run away, disobey God, and not go and give the Word of the Lord to these wicked people.

I'm sure you've already heard or read about Jonah and the whale, so let's move to the heart of the story. Jonah eventually ended up on the streets of Nineveh. In Jonah 3:4 he proclaimed, "Forty more days, and Nineveh will be overthrown," and here's what happened.

The Ninevites believed God. They declared a fast, and all of them from the greatest to the least put on sackcloth. When the news reached the King of Nineveh, he rose from his throne, took off his royal robes, covered himself with sackcloth, and sat down in the dust.

Then he issued a proclamation in Nineveh: "By the decree of the king and his nobles: Do not let any man, beast, herd, or flock taste a thing. Do not let them eat or drink water, but let man and beast be covered with sackcloth, and let everyone call out mightily to God. Let everyone turn from his evil ways and from the violence that is in his hands. Who knows? God may yet relent, and with compassion turn from his fierce anger so that we will not perish" (Jonah 3:7–9).

When God saw what they did and how they had turned from their evil ways, He had compassion and didn't bring upon them the destruction He had threatened. God stayed His anger. He looked into the hearts of the people of Nineveh and saw repentant hearts.

Jonah said to the Lord, "... That's why I fled previously to Tarshish, because I knew you're a compassionate God, slow to anger, and overflowing with gracious love, and reluctant to send trouble" (Jonah 4:2).

Do you fully understand the implications of what is being said here, saints? God changed His mind and decided to show His forgiveness and love because the people heeded the call to repent.

This Old Testament God showed this compassion, the same God who destroyed Egypt, Jericho, Babylon, the Medes, and Persians, along with Sodom and Gomorrah. If the saints of God would use Nineveh as a template for America, God would also intervene on our behalf, because how much more would He be willing to answer our cry for mercy through Jesus Christ?

CHAPTER 6

A Strong Delusion

Religion has suddenly become a crutch for the deluded masses, so much so that it has become almost a fanatical insanity. Religion does not lead to a relationship with the God of the Bible; it leads to a relationship with the god of this world.

As I have previously stated, religion is the blood that pumps through Satan's veins. It is his life force that confuses humanity into thinking that the way to have a relationship with God is through the teachings of man, teachings that are inspired by hell itself. Youtube has become an end-time video buffet for end-time religious charlatans.

These con artists cling to religious teachings and the opinions of other false teachers on what they believe will transpire before our Lord returns. Just as God's Word proclaims, God has sent a strong delusion upon these end-time money changers because they neglect the knowledge of the truth that is clearly found in His Word.

They shout from the pulpits in America, "Fear not, Church. God is going to rapture you away and take you to eternal bliss while the rest of the world suffers through tribulation and judgment." However, they forget that judgment begins in the house of God.

I believe that if Christians would spend a lot more time really studying the Bible for themselves instead of following teachings that have been passed down from man over the last few decades, we might be forced to face the truth.

Here's a thought. If the Bible teaches what these false prophets want you to believe, then we will be raptured away before a seven-year tribulation and the advent of the antichrist. Why then do the one hundred forty-four thousand who are spoken about in the Book of Revelation still remain on Earth during this time? Why don't they go up in this rapture of believers?

I'm sure they have been believers for a long time; the Bible makes it clear that they are without sin. In Revelation 7, they're called "servants of our God." Yet they're here during the time of Jacob's trouble.

The time of Jacob's trouble is a quote from Jeremiah 30:7, which references the tribulation period. These one hundred forty-four thousand servants of God will preach and proclaim His Word during the middle of the tribulation.

Maybe these one hundred forty-four thousand have to proclaim God's Word because of the Church's failure to do so, the Church that thinks they have the right to be rescued for doing nothing. Sorry, folks. Don't believe the fairytale that God is going to rescue a cold, dead Church. If anything, He'll put the Church through the fire so that He can refine and redeem it from its own mediocrity and prosperity gospel.

Ouch! The truth cuts like a knife, does it not. Much of what we hear and see, whether it's on television, radio, or the Internet is intentionally generated by false prophets, false teachers, and religious globalists and not true believers. They're causing confusion in the minds of those who are sincerely seeking the truth of the Bible. They're trying to cripple and destabilize true believers through a mass deception of truth.

These false teachings on end-time events draw true Christians into a false security. In essence, they become spiritual zombies running to hear messages of health, wealth, and security. They're unable to make sense of anything they hear from these teachers. They become ripe for deception. Some of them even jumped on the Mayan calendar's December 21, 2012, bandwagon proclaiming that the earth would end on that day like it was a scripture being fulfilled.

It's sad to watch true believers run with itching ears from one teacher to another, wanting to hear how they'll escape the coming trouble. Their faith in God has dried up at its root. They have no desire to hear the truth but only what puts their minds at ease. They don't want to stand and fight for their beliefs. They want to be rescued and delivered as if it's owed to them.

In addition, when they do hear the truth or see someone who is on fire for God and proclaiming His truth, they label him as a nut or fanatic. On the other hand, they can go to a football game or concert, make fools of themselves in front of the whole world, and act like its normal.

We've become accustomed to this lukewarm way of thinking and teaching and have let wolves come in to preach and control our congregations. We're living a fake life and have a fake relationship with the Christ of the cross.

2 Thessalonians 2:11–12 says, "And for this cause God shall send them strong delusion, that they should believe a lie: That they all might be damned who believed not the truth, but had pleasure in unrighteousness."

This is it, folks. We are the last generation before the return of Christ. We're the generation of accountability that will stand before Him for the way we voted. Did we act on God's moral law or man's?

God will require that each and every one of us give account for what we believe and what we have allowed ourselves to believe, no matter who the teachers were. We are required to seek and search and understand the Bible and not depend on the teachings of men.

It's our responsibility to seek out the truth of God's Word. If we miss it, we have no one to blame but ourselves. Jesus said He would send the Comforter to teach and guide us into a loving relationship with our Creator. The Comforter would teach us all truth and show us things to come.

The Church has grown so far from a true relationship with God that we have become accustomed to being controlled by religious half-truths and false teachers who have lost faith in the Bible. We're like sheep being led to the slaughter. Additionally, because of our weakness and loss of real faith in this generation, the Church in America and America itself will fall under the chastisement of God.

You think I enjoy proclaiming this truth? This is a fearful and terrible message, not something that people want to hear. I must give account for these words and this message. I'd rather tell the truth for fear of God than proclaim a lie with the praise of men. I have been guilty of living that way in the past.

Our only hope for America and the Church is true-heart repentance. I'm talking about a repentance of weeping and fasting, forsaking the love of this world and this life, and refocusing our attention on the God of heaven. As the '70s song by the band Kansas says, we're just dust in the wind.

Moreover, if we're lucky we might live seventy years. As we came into this world with nothing, we leave it with nothing except for the love we gave to others and the lives we touched with that love.

Especially in this generation, we have spent most of our life as slaves to the power of the airwaves. Satan, the master deceiver and the prince of the power of the air, has enticed us into a zombie-like slumber through movies, television, Internet, radio, cell phones, and video games. I'm not saying you can't enjoy these technological advances. I'm saying for you to know how to keep it under subjection and to have balance.

Don't let these things control you, but you control them and have enough common sense to walk away if it becomes controlling. We have become a generation of technological addicts, feeding the agenda of Satan whose one and only desire is to destroy man.

> *And you hath he quickened, who were dead in trespasses and sins; Wherein times past ye walked according to the course of this world, according to the prince of the power of the air, the spirit that now worketh in the children of disobedience: Among whom also we all had our conversation in times past in the lusts of our flesh, fulfilling the desires of the flesh and of the mind;*

and were by nature the children of wrath, even as others (Ephesians 2:1–3).

This generation is the children of disobedience. We live to fulfill the desires of our flesh and mind while we totally disregard the gospel of Christ. The biggest insult to God is that we sit in our pulpits expecting a rapture for our apostasy.

Satan has planted so many deceivers in the Church that we've become mesmerized by any new trend that comes along. We watch as professed men of God rise from total obscurity and proclaim a new-age gospel that's supposed to be purpose driven. They then set themselves up as the voice of the Church to rub shoulders with politicians and global elitist who make and pass laws that spit in the face of Almighty God.

If these were real men of God, they would proclaim to these leaders to repent and seek God's face for their violation of His Word and the killing of the innocent babies ripped apart every day in their mother's womb.

Do you really think they care about preaching the real gospel? They are in it for the notoriety, the fame, and the fortune. I'm of the opinion that if Christ came today preaching the gospel He preached two thousand years ago, the politicians in this country would have Him put to death. The Church would be shouting, "Crucify Him!"

Our Lord is blasphemed daily. The Church does nothing but watch as this country slips into an abyss of eternal damnation. Churches are now ordaining homosexuals and supporting abortion rights, all in the name of compromise. To make matters even worse, we vote for politicians who enact and pass laws that totally violate God's Word.

Afterward, we watch as they destroy the Christian roots of our nation.

I'm baffled by the thousands of ministries that hit the airwaves every week asking for donations to either save their ministry or provide aid to people in foreign countries. In the meantime, our own country is dying spiritually and financially.

America is doomed if the Church does not repent and call for our leaders and our nation to repent. God will destroy this nation, and it will go the way of all nations that had turned its back on a Holy God.

If God didn't spare the Jews who were given the very oracles of God, what makes you think He won't destroy this nation? The God of the Old Testament is alive and well, so don't think your white-washed Christianity is going to deter His wrath for your violation of His Word. He is the same yesterday, today, and forever.

Judgment will come, and it will begin with the Church. Think on this, my brothers and sisters. You believe that God won't let anything happen to the Church, right? The God of our Father Abraham, the God of the Jews, allowed Hitler to murder six million of His chosen people just less than eighty years ago. What makes us think we should fare any better than they did?

A new evil has been born in the Church, a deception that has blinded the most devout believers. A do-nothing and who-cares attitude is escalating. A let's eat-drink-and-be-merry mentality is thriving while the country is destroyed by satanically inspired politicians. They're very easy to identify because they are without common sense. They're self-indulgent egomaniacs, and their one-and-only desire is to heap treasures upon themselves that are taken off of the backs of the middle class. In addition, like true hypocrites, they try to maintain a form of godliness but deny the power of God.

For some ungodly reason, the Church today thinks that if you don't fall into line with their respective teachings, you're a hell-bound heathen. Most of these teachings that are regurgitated from the pulpit on a weekly basis leave so many unanswered questions that the people walk around in confusion.

I've spoken to many pastors and teachers and called them out on some of these errant teachings and doctrines. Their answer to me is "We know you're right, but to maintain order within the church and to stand by our bylaws and beliefs, we must teach these things to keep the people coming in."

The result of getting out-of-step with what they teach and believe is acquiring the label of a heretic or Judas. They'll discredit you and expel you from their church and make sure everyone knows you're acting in rebellion and against their beliefs.

What has gone wrong? Why is there such hatred against anyone who tries to tell the truth or warn against the judgment of God?

Satan has limited time. He knows his time is short. Just as he deceived a third of heaven's angels who lived in the very presence of God, he has caused a greater deception to fall upon the Church. We have fallen for it hook, line, and sinker. The Pharisees and Sadducees were guilty of not being able to discern and wrongly interpret the prophetic signs that were all around them at the first coming of our Lord. Just like them, we have become guilty of wrongly interpreting the prophetic signs of His second coming.

The religious Jews were expecting a Messiah who

would overthrow the Romans, set Himself up as King, and lead them out of foreign domination. Instead, a Messiah came and labeled them hypocrites and charlatans. He rebuked them for their false teachings and deception of the people.

"And He found in the temple those who were selling oxen and sheep and doves, and the money changers seated at their tables. And He made a scourge of cords, and drove them all out of the temple, with the sheep and the oxen; and He poured out the coins of the money changers and overturned their tables;" (John 2:14–15). Jesus confronted them in the temple for turning God's house into a house of profit.

Sound familiar? History is repeating itself in the Church today. The grafted-in branches have let the root of that same evil corrupt the tree.

Jesus accused the religious Jews of meting out laws for the people to obey, yet they wouldn't obey them. They used these laws to control the people and to keep the people under subjection and subordinate to their false teaching.

The only hope for the Church is turning back to God with true repentance. If we get back to our first love, we have the potential and the power to not only change the Church, but the world as well.

What has gone wrong is that we've become like fatted calves ready to be slaughtered. We have eaten and fed our minds on the lie that we will never face trouble here in America. We are the elect who will be whisked away before judgment fall s. We believe that God wants to deliver us from the persecution we face here every day. What He will deliver us from are our fancy homes and cars, our boats and jet skis, our golf tournaments and video games, our vacations and vacation homes, our ski trips and fancy restaurants, our investments and retirement packages, our soft church pews, and our luxurious church buildings, and all of our name-it-claim-it mentality.

Yes, no trouble, no hard times, and no judgment for us. We have the rapture to save us.

I pray that true men of God will arise in this generation to proclaim the living truth of God's Word. It's time for us to get back on track and return to our first love. We have fallen so in love with the world, and along the way, we've forgotten how to love God.

I long to see revival. It's my heart's desire to see men with the faith that can move mountains, faith that causes the world to cry out to God for salvation, healing, and restoration.

Could you imagine what the reaction of the world would be if someone with no legs was prayed for, and new legs were actually formed before their very eyes? What about someone who was dead for three days and raised back to life? How about the deaf hearing and the blind seeing? If this could just happen in one church in America every day, it would change everything. It would hit every news outlet within hours. Instead, we have become accustomed to seeing the phonies play out the same circus act every week before they ask us for our money.

I know this is harsh, but you know as well as I do that it's all true. I don't like writing this information, but I have to do so. The Spirit of God compels me to proclaim the truth. Maybe it will cause some of you to get angry enough to do something about it. Maybe it will help you pray more, fast more, or put down the love of this world and to seek the face of God.

Just like you, I deal with my own humanity every day. As long as we're doing something to try to change, though, it's better than doing nothing.

Jesus said that the greatest commandment was to love the Lord thy God with all of your heart, mind, and strength (Matthew 22:37). It's up to us to change ourselves before we try to change others.

Daniel was grieved over the spiritual decline that he witnessed in Israel. He lamented over how they had turned their backs on God as both a nation and a people. He sought God through persistent prayer. Daniel never gave up even when he was commanded not to pray under the threat of death. He thought it better to obey the laws of God instead of the laws of men. He could not and would not submit himself to any leadership that would take away his fundamental rights to live for and serve the God in whom he believed. Yet in the Church today, we let this nation's leaders tell us that we can't pray in our schools and in any other place where we might offend certain special-interest groups.

We've become so fearful of government and lawsuits that we refuse to preach or speak anything negative. We want to give in because of fear despite the fact that we have a biblical record of divine providence and protection that He promised to give us in His Word. Nevertheless, we don't trust the Bible or have enough faith to take a stand against the tyranny within the leadership of this nation.

We have to turn back. We have to repent and get desperate for God. We have to quit closing our ears to the Holy Spirit and reclaim our nation for the glory of God. We have to get back to the streets, back into the highways and byways and preach an Old Testament gospel with a New Testament grace.

Let's forget about building new churches. Let's forget this feel-good prosperity message of love and butterflies and get back to the God of fire, the God who parted oceans for His people to escape, the God who walked in the fiery furnace to save His anointed ones, the God who shut the mouths of lions and raised the dead, and the God who sends famine and protects and provides for His people. Let's get back to the God who fed six-million people as they wandered in the wilderness, delivering them from the slavery of a nation that defied the God in which they believed and hoped. Let's focus on the God who, in His great compassion, love, and mercy, sent His one and only Son to die for the sins of fallen men.

He will deliver us from our nation's sins if we turn and trust in Him. He will in His mercy turn our nation back unto Himself, but it has to start with us first. He must lay the axe at the root of the Church so that He can cut the corruption of the world out of our lives.

All over the planet, men and women of God are having visions and dreams of the destruction of America. It's a warning of what will come to pass if America continues on the path it has chosen and if the Church does not call for its people or the nation to repent. Because of this, the blood of the innocent will be the responsibility of those who knew the truth and did nothing.

The Church is the watchman to the world. Has it warned or has it comforted those who have broken faith with God?

If you our reading this and you know God's Word, you know everything I have said is true. If you deny these truths, then you're a liar and a deceiver. Remember this, the God of the New Testament, who you water down as weak and full of love, returns and slaughters millions in the valley of Megiddo. It says the blood will flow up to the bridal of a horse.

That Old Testament God is alive and well and will make it known very soon.

Mene, Mene, Tekel, Parsin

The King of Babylon had decided to set himself up against the Lord of heaven. In the pride of his heart, he disregarded God's law.

God's message was "… Mene: I have numbered the days of your reign and brought it to an end.

"Tekel: You have been weighed on the scales and found wanting.

"Parsin: Your kingdom is divided and given to the Medes and Persians" (Daniel 5:26–28).

The similarities between the Babylon mentioned in the Book of Revelation and America are too real to be coincidental. The similarities between the Medes and the Persians, which are Iran and Iraq, are also too real to be coincidental in such a time as this. This is especially true when America and her leaders have set themselves up against God's laws and the principles of our forefathers who dedicated this nation to God.

With that in mind, the Spirit of the Lord gave me this message for His people, His land, and its wicked leaders, and to those who have tried to oppose His laws and violate His covenants. This message is for those who have murdered the unborn and who make laws, calling good evil and evil good.

In Jeremiah 2:5–6, the Lord says, "What fault did your ancestors find in me, that they strayed so far from me? They followed worthless idols [money, fame, notoriety, pride, rebellion, religion, and false gods] and became worthless themselves. They did not ask, 'Where is the Lord, who brought us up out of Egypt and led us through the barren wilderness, through a land of deserts and ravines, a land of drought and darkness, a land where no one travels and no one lives.'"

For America, Egypt represents the tyranny under which Christians lived before they came to here. For America, this represents the untraveled ocean that separated Europe from its borders, which was a place of uncertain darkness for those who traveled by sea. At the time, it was believed that the world was flat and that they would sail off the edge of the world.

"'I brought you into a fertile land to eat its fruit and rich produce. But you came and defiled my land and made my inheritance detestable. The priests did not ask, "Where is the Lord?" Those who deal with the law did not know me; the leaders rebelled against me. The prophets prophesied by Baal, following worthless idols. Therefore, I bring charges against you again,' declares the Lord" (Jeremiah 2:7–9).

"'Has a nation ever changed its gods? (Yet they are not gods at all). But my people have exchanged their glorious God for worthless idols. Be appalled at this, you heavens, and shudder with great horror,' declares the Lord" (Jeremiah 2:11–12).

His Word to me was "My people, this nation has committed sins that have reached the heavens. In the pride of their heart they say there is no God. I pled with them with earthquakes, tornados, fire, drought, and storms, but they continually make laws that violate my laws. They call wicked good and good wicked. They have become ministers of deception. They tax my people into slavery so that they can live in comfort and ease. Then they use their power to enact legislation that opposes My will.

"They rob my people of their God-given rights so as to crush their spirit and cause them hurt and despair. They lie, cheat their way into power, and use their positions to destroy the history of their forefathers and call it moral evolution.

"I, the Lord, the God of all humanity, am sending warnings and harbingers. Yet My people, those who say they are Mine, do nothing to bring forth fruits worthy of repentance. They say. 'Eat, drink, and be merry because we are chosen to escape.'

"You shall not escape," says the Lord of host. "Judgment will begin in My house first. You shall taste the chastisement of a living God, and none shall escape in this generation.

"I am returning soon. Repent and seek my face. It will be a day of judgment and despair, a day of weeping and travail, a day when I will require you to stand before Me in judgment for doing nothing with the word I gave you. You were to be a light to the world, but instead you have become a prostitute to the nations.

"Those, My servants who have made themselves white and have refrained from the pleasures of the world, you shall rule and reign at My return. I will exalt you and lift you up for keeping faith with your God. You shall be crowned with glory and honor, and you shall live forever in the presence of your Lord and God.

"Have you not brought this on yourselves by forsaking the Lord your God when He led you in the way? Your wickedness shall punish you; your backsliding will rebuke you. Consider then and realize how evil and bitter it is for you when you forsake your God and have no awe of Me," declares the Lord, the Lord Almighty.

"You broke off your yoke and tore off your bonds. You said, 'I will not serve the Lord.' Why do you bring charges against me? You have all rebelled against me," declares the Lord. "You, of this generation, consider the Word of the Lord. You have forgotten me days without number. How skilled you are at pursuing sin. Even the worst of sinners can learn from you. Yet in spite of all this, you say, 'I am innocent. God is not angry with me.' But I will pass judgment on you because you say 'I have not sinned.' You have defiled your land with your wickedness and caused disgrace to My house through your love of money.

"Repent, for I will frown on you no longer, for I am merciful," declares the Lord. "I will not be angry forever. Only acknowledge your guilt. You have rebelled against the Lord your God who called you. Return faithless people," says the Lord, "for I am your God. Repent, for the wickedness of this people is great. Return, and I will give you shepherds after My own heart who will lead you with knowledge and understanding.

"How gladly would I treat you like sons and make you once again a desirable land, the most beautiful inheritance next to my son Israel. I thought you would call Me Father and not turn away from following Me. But like a woman unfaithful to her husband, you have been unfaithful to me.

"Crying is heard, a great weeping and pleading for this obstinate nation because you have perverted your ways and have rejected and forgotten the Lord your God. Return, faithless nation, and I will cure you of your backsliding. Be not deceived. You will reap what you have sown.

"Lie down in shame, and let disgrace cover the sinner.

This people have sinned against the Lord God greatly in this generation. America, if you will return to the Lord God, if you put an end to your violence and idolatry and no longer go astray, and if you in truth and justice in a righteous way return unto your rock, then I will in return leave a blessing and not a curse.

"Break up your unplowed ground, sow, and sin no more. Circumcise yourselves to the Lord. Circumcise your heart, rebellious nation, or My wrath will break out and burn like fire because of the evil and wickedness you have done. Return to Me. Call for weeping and fasting. Seek the face of the Lord your God, or I will pounce upon you like a lion on its prey.

"A destroyer of nations has risen. He has come out of his dwelling place. He brings terrible devastation and disaster to an obstinate and rebellious people.

"The earth shakes in fear. The heavens become like brass for great is the wrath of Him who sits on the throne of judgment. He has left His place to lay waste to your land. Your towns will be in ruins without inhabitants. Repent and cry out before the fierce anger of the Lord breaks out upon your people and upon your land.

"Am I not the God who is the same yesterday, today, and forever? In your pride and arrogance, what makes you believe you can escape my judgment and loving chastisement? In the day I do these things shall you not see and believe that I am the living God, a God who relents in sending disaster if My people will just repent and turn from their wickedness.

"In that day," declares the Lord, "your president and your politicians will lose heart. Your priests and preachers will be horrified at the disaster I will bring upon an unrepentant people. Woe to you; you will be ruined. Wash the evil from your heart and be saved.

"How long will you rebel against the Lord? Have you not chosen this path for your nation and its people? You pride yourself on sending aid to others while you deny justice to your own people. Your own conduct and actions against Me have brought all these things upon you. I will pierce your heart with My judgments. How bitter it will be for you in those days. You will writhe in pain and anguish. No man, no nation, no politics, and no people will save you on the day of the Lord's judgment.

"My people are fools; they do not follow Me. They are senseless children; they only understand evil. They only do good to exalt pride and rebellion. Repent of this," says the Lord.

"The whole land will I ruin, but I will not completely destroy it. I have a remnant here, those who call on the Lord and seek His council. They walk in faith before the Lord. They cry out to Him for mercy. They are My treasure who I will protect under the shadow of My presence. I am with them; they are my people, and I am their God. They shall rule and reign in the Kingdom that comes.

"The earth will mourn as you cry out in anguish, and the heavens will grow dark from your punishment, you who sit as queen to the nations. Your rebellion and sorceries will be no more in days to come.

"You thought in the pride of your heart that no harm would come to your shores. You thought in the pride of your heart that the sword would never be raised in your nation. You thought in the pride of your heart that the Lord God would overlook your sin and bless you because of good works.

"But hear this, you foolish and senseless people who have eyes but do not see, who have ears but do not hear. Should you not fear the Lord? Did not your forefathers fear me? Did they not dedicate this nation to My glory? Did I not save them from their enemies and make this a great nation?

"You have violated the covenants they made with Me. You have transgressed and sinned against everything for which they gave their lives. You have broken faith with your own people and put a yoke of bondage on their backs while living in luxury. You have sinned against the land and its people. You impose laws that you yourself do not obey and then make the people bear the burden of your rebellion. In trust, they elected you, and you destroy them with lies. Should you not fear the Lord? Have you not learned from the nations you rule over that God has blessed you?

"Now the Lord Himself shall destroy the pride of your rebellion. He will cause your own people to rise against you. They will be My instrument of judgment against your rebellious heart. I will whistle for your enemies to help them. I will call vultures to feast on your carcasses for your defiance against the one true God.

"Fear the Lord, for great and mighty is the God who established this nation. On the prayers of your forefathers, they will rise in judgment against this generation for profaning the God of glory. Your wrongdoings have kept My blessing away; your sins have deprived you of the good I want to do. This people elects wicked men. You become snared like a bird in a cage to their broken promises and lies. They lie in wait to deceive you. They lie in wait to destroy you. They become rich and powerful. They fatten themselves on the choicest morsels of division, and their evil deeds have no limit. They do not plead for the poor or orphans, and they rob from the old and steal from the young for power and greed.

"Should I not punish them for this?" declares the Lord. "Should I not avenge myself on a nation such as this? A horrible and shocking thing has happened in America. Priests, politicians, and prophets proclaim lies. They all rule by their own authority, and my people love it that way."

This is what the Maker of heaven and earth says: "You stand at the crossroads. Now look. Return unto the faith of your forefathers. Walk in the way I called you, and you will find forgiveness and rest. But you have said, 'We will not walk in those ways. We have evolved high above God's laws.'

"Did not I set watchmen over you, but in the pride of your own glory you refuse to obey? Therefore listen, obstinate people. Hear all the earth. Disaster upon disaster will overtake you. You shall reap the fruit of your schemes because you have turned your back on the Lord who can save you. I will put obstacles before you. Mighty men and politicians shall stumble. The people shall perish because of willful ignorance, for they have received the knowledge of the truth, but they mock it.

"Consider this," says the Lord. "Am I not a merciful and just God? Did you not walk in My blessing when you followed in My ways? Did not the people of the earth fear your greatness because of My love for you?

"I made you a light to the nations. You were my daughter who I exalted before other nations. They admired your beauty and elegance, and they longed for your embrace. Why have you turned from your Father, the God who saves? You have whored out your people for power.

"You make them slaves to your rebellion and kill their children with your laws. I hear the screams of the innocent.

Their blood cries out to me. They will rise up to judge you, and you shall not escape. From the poor to the rich, from the least to the greatest, to the prophet to the priest, all will be held accountable for the murder of the unborn. Those who call it a women's right to choose, who are you, dust of the earth, that you think you can choose life or death? I am God, and beside me, there is no other.

"You think yourselves gods, then you save yourselves from My forthcoming wrath. You shall lie like dung on the earth on the day that I judge you. Repent, and who knows the mind of the Lord? I will show mercy on that day if you turn back to Me.

"Great is the Lord who created man in His image. He is slow to anger and abounds in tender mercy. He longs for His people to repent. Even in judgment He shows compassion. You are living in deception. In your own deceit you refuse to acknowledge Me.

"Beware," says the Lord. "Do not trust friend or brother, for they are a brood of deceivers and slanderers. They will testify against you. They use you for their own gain, and it is I the Lord who will use them to judge you."

CHAPTER 7

Trusting God

"You have said harsh things against me," says the LORD. "Yet you ask, 'What have we said against you?' You have said, 'It is futile to serve God. What did we gain by carrying out his requirements and going about like mourners before the LORD Almighty? But now we call the arrogant blessed. Certainly the evildoers prosper, and even those who challenge God escape.' Then those who feared the LORD talked with each other, and the LORD listened and heard. A scroll of remembrance was written in his presence concerning those who feared the LORD and honored his name. "They will be mine," says the LORD Almighty, "in the day when I make up my treasured possession. I will spare them, just as in compassion a man spares his son who serves him. And you will again see the distinction between the righteous and the wicked,

> *between those who serve God and those who do not"*
> (Malachi 3:13–18).

I won't lie to you; it's very difficult to trust in God sometimes. He has not allowed life to be easy for most of us.

You get up praying. You continuously pray during the day, and when evening comes, you go to bed praying the same prayer day after day, week after week, month after month, and year after year. You have that hope within you that maybe this will be the day when God answers your prayers. Then every night you go to bed disappointed that another day has gone by and nothing has changed.

Where is the God who said He loves me? Where is the God who said He would never leave me nor forsake me? Where is the God who said I came that you might have life and have it more abundantly?

You begin to get angry, and you become envious of all of the Hollywood elites who seem to live under the shadow of His blessing everyday while they live their lives as if God doesn't exist. You see the worst of humanity getting everything their hearts desire without praying a single prayer while you struggle just to make ends meet, begging God every day for just one break.

However, who am I to question how God handles His affairs with men? Do I like it? I give a resounding *no*. It's a big letdown. Period.

Therefore, I began to question God on this matter. I wanted to know about His justice on this. I wanted to know why evil men were being blessed while all of the hopes and prayers of His servants were being crushed.

His response changed my whole view of how things are. He said, "Paul, did you ever stop to think that this life is the only heaven some will ever know, a man-made heaven based on worldly pleasures? Did you ever stop to think that this life might be the only hell my servants will ever know, based on human standards?"

Now which is better, the pleasures of the world for maybe eighty years or the pleasures of heaven in the warm embrace of your Father's love for all eternity? We've been put in this world to be watchmen, to sound the alarm and warn the people of the upcoming judgment if they continue to reject His plan of redemption.

We have the knowledge and the information to pull them from the fire. God has chosen this generation to fulfill the prophecies of His Word, yet we're distracted by the world and its pleasures, which will soon fade away.

The prophets of the Old Testament were the watchmen for their generation. When the Spirit of God came upon them, He showed them His judgments over those nations that chose to rebel, including Israel. They saw that He might send pestilence, drought, famine, and/or devastating earthquakes. They might have seen invading armies wiping out their people and killing everything in their path.

These prophets chose to live a life free from the influence of the world so that they might not be stained by the sin of its pleasure. Their warnings were full of loud emotion and terror in order to incite the people into a reverent fear of God Almighty.

Can you picture in your mind what these men could have looked like? Can you see their long sad faces with long hair and a beard down to their belly buttons and maybe a staff in their hands, looking like crazed madmen shouting warnings and woes. Yet they were normal, full of the love, compassion, and mercy of the living God. He chose men like these because He saw the attributes of His Spirit within them.

With excitement and exuberance, they were willing to warn the people in love. They lived to shout and proclaim God's judgments so that the people would turn to Him for mercy. They looked forward to the day when the Messiah would come and provide redemption back to God. They lived and breathed that message.

We have a responsibility in this generation as men and women of God to testify about His great mercy and loving kindness as well as about His fierce anger and wrath toward the disobedient. This generation needs to show some tenacity about the Holiness of God and living a life that's separate from worldly pleasures.

I'm not saying that we have to walk around like stiff-necked nannies calling everything sin. I'm talking only about what the Bible says regarding moral absolutes.

A watchman's job in biblical days was to stand on the wall in a high place and describe to the people what he saw coming. Maybe he could see an invading army a distance away, or maybe a bad storm approaching, or maybe thieves and robbers outside the gates. He had the responsibility to warn the people not to go beyond the walls if he saw danger in any way. If he saw any threat and didn't say anything, he alone would be held responsible for whatever occurred as a result.

A servant of God is a watchman. We are the ones who God will hold responsible for not warning the people about what's on the way. We know God's view of what's taking place in this nation because His Word makes it perfectly clear to us. History teaches us what God does to those who refuse to follow His law but instead follow their own ways.

Christians today don't believe in the Old Testament God. They are deluded into believing that God overlooks their sin and the sin of the people because of grace. Not true at all, my friends.

God is not going to be mocked because of grace. Just because some Old Testament prophet isn't predicting apocalyptic judgments on the earth doesn't mean God's unaware of the sin of the people. Don't think He'll continue to let His people make a mockery of the cross and His Word through their willful disobedience of doing nothing.

There's a storm coming, a devastating storm of destruction if God's people, His watchmen to this generation, don't quit using His grace as a license to do nothing. We the people have settled ourselves into such mediocrity that we don't even act shocked when the President of the United States puts the final nail in the coffin of the American family.

Our former president openly supported gay marriage. Then he had the nerve to call himself a Christian after he ran his whole presidential race proclaiming he believed in the biblical definition of marriage. A Christian knows the Word of God and what God says about homosexual behavior. At one of the most pivotal points in American history, we elected a president who prostituted himself out to the Hollywood elite for political donations so that we the people would vote him back into office.

Where are the watchmen? Have they never read the biblical story of Sodom and Gomorrah? You think God doesn't see and hear the obstinacy of the people, they who pass these satanic laws and spit in the face of God Almighty? Have we gone mad in America?

I mean, really. All of the things that the Bible calls sin, America promotes as a human right protected by government oversight. Think about it, saints. Look at what has happened in this country because of our sleep and slumber. We're now facing the judgment of a living God, and what do we do? We vote God's enemies back into political office.

Where are those who have been called to warn the people? Those who claim to be Christians are silent. They say God is love, and as long as there is love involved, it's all good.

Look, I won't lie to you. I do things that stay between God and me, personal things that I have a biblical right to do. But because I believe they would cause some believers to stumble or be offended, I keep these things to myself.

The Bible says I have a responsibility not to do or let people see me do those things because to some, it might be sin. However, as a believer, the Bible calls me blessed because I am not condemned for the things that I allow.

I mentioned this in a prior chapter, but the Bible is specific about moral absolutes. As believers, we know what these moral absolutes are. The Word of God makes it perfectly clear as to what God does to a people who allow this kind of lifestyle. This nation will now reap the results of allowing men to marry men and voting in leaders who make laws protecting the rights of these men.

Watchmen, you who sit on the walls and do nothing, your God and Lord is coming soon. You will be held accountable for your lack of action. Why do you prophesy lies to the people? You promise wealth for obeying the Old

Testament law of tithing, yet you forget the laws of God regarding sodomy.

Where is the outrage of those who call themselves Christians? Where is the passion for your faith? Blood will be upon your head, the blood of the unborn who you murdered and the blood of those God judges. Your own inactions will condemn you. You have a form of godliness, yet your love of pleasure outweighs your love for God.

You say, "Lord, how are we guilty? We didn't participate in the sins of these people."

Did you put as much time in warning the people as you did in seeking out worldly pleasures? Did you tell them God loves them and to turn from sin, or did you tell them God loves them and keep sinning because of grace? Grace is not a license to sin. It's there to show God's love, mercy, and compassion to those who turn away from sin.

If we the people could choose the right path and turn back to God, then He could and would restore health and prosperity to our nation. He would heal our self-inflicted wounds and cure us of our own rebellion.

America is committing suicide every time we enact laws that violate His laws. We have a justice system that can and will convict people for crimes based on circumstantial evidence. While at the same time, though, we don't have enough common sense to understand that all of the things that have happened in this country over the last fifty years are because we have decided not to believe in the Bible anymore. Still, we consider all of these end-time events as negligible, even though they go beyond circumstantial because we witness them every day. Don't they point out to us that God is displeased with this people and its leaders?

We have leaders who proclaim America is no longer a Christian nation, and we keep silent. Are you kidding me! God is giving us leaders who are raping and killing our nation, and it's because we the people turn a blind eye.

Think about it, Church. If what we did today was done fifty years ago, most of our politicians and most of Hollywood would be behind bars or executed for treason. Still we call it a divine evolution of change for the better. Honestly, what is getting better?

I see things getting worse and worse every day. How has this evolution worked out for you?

God is calling us to turn back, and we must heed His warning. It's our only hope. God longs for us to return to Him so that He might show us His great love and mercy.

"Like as I have brought all this great evil upon this people, so will I bring upon them all the good that I have promised them" (Jeremiah 32:42).

God will show love and mercy in judgment, but we must turn back to Him. Just as surely as God's Word tells you that judgment must come, it also tells you that repentance will bring goodness, grace, and mercy.

As watchmen, we have to put our trust in God, and we also must not become obsessed with doom and gloom. We have one responsibility, which is to warn and alert people of what is coming as a result of breaking God's law. All of these, though, must be confirmed by scripture. We're to gain knowledge from scripture and pray regarding how to warn the people about the impending storm of judgment so that we can prepare our own hearts for whatever God's judgment brings.

Just remember that numerous times in biblical history, great men of God survived when their nations were destroyed and invaded by foreign powers. They were taken off into exile, never to see their nation again. However, they survived and even thrived under the worst of these circumstances.

So, don't let fear or anxieties consume you. Let the Spirit of God dominate your mind and guide your heart.

Darkness will come; it's inevitable. God has to judge a nation that turns away from Him. His justice won't permit Him to look away. It might be delayed, but it will come.

True believers have nothing to fear. The Bible also makes it perfectly clear that God can't judge the wicked unless He protects the righteous. The blood of Jesus Christ protects us from the wrath of God and His judgment of the wicked.

Satan wants you to live in fear. His aphrodisiac is your fear created by seeing everything crumbling around us. He'll take you to another extreme by driving you to a place of doubt and hopelessness. He loves to cause confusion. He'll try to rob you of your faith with thoughts of helplessness and insecurities of who you are in Christ. But he fears your faith more than you fear him. So, if he can cause you to lose your trust and hope in God, he wins.

Of course, he can never have you unless you let him. Nevertheless, if he robs you of your faith, you become powerless in God's army. When that happens, it's because he has pierced your armor and penetrated a weakness, making you ineffective.

"Finally, brethren, whatsoever things are true, whatsoever things are honest, whatsoever things are just, whatsoever things are pure, whatsoever things are lovely, whatsoever things are of good report; if there be any virtue, and if there be any praise, think on these things" (Philippians 4:8).

Listen child of God, with all of these warnings, take heed and be obedient to God's Word. Fix your thoughts on Christ and His coming. Keep your armor tightly secured, and if you stumble, don't lie there. Get up and keep fighting because as God's Word proclaims, "… greater is He who is in you than he who is in the world" (1 John 4:4).

We are more than conquerors, saints. The signs of the times are pointing to a change in America, to the lifestyle of her people, and to all of the nations that God has prospered. It's already happening all over the world.

There is a rapid change in the balance of power. God will use a nation of His choice to judge another for the sins of its leaders. America is not exempt.

When will these events take place? God has not yet revealed the timing. However, He has revealed that He's giving the Church time to prepare, to get her oil for its lamps, and to warn the people of what's to come if there's no repentance.

God has promised us that He will keep us in perfect peace if we keep our thoughts on Him and trust in Him (Isaiah 26:3). Is your heart secure in Him? Are you at peace, even though you know what will come to a rebellious people? We don't have to live in fear, saints, for we have applied the blood of our Lord and God's Christ to our lives.

I think of all of the great stories in the Bible, and the one I love most is the story of the fiery furnace. There's a lot to the story, but I'll just cover some of it to make my point.

In Daniel chapters 2 and 3, Daniel goes before King Nebuchadnezzar as God's liaison to reveal to him the meaning of a dream that caused the king a great deal of concern. The prophetic dream was about his kingdom and the kingdoms of the future.

In the king's dream, he saw a large statue that Daniel described as awesome in appearance. The head was made of pure gold, its chest and arms of silver, its belly and thighs of bronze, its legs of iron, and its feet partly of iron and partly of baked clay.

Because of this dream, King Nebuchadnezzar decided he would make an image of gold ninety feet high and nine feet wide and set it up in one of his provinces in Babylon. When it was ready, he summoned all of the members of his provincial government to come to a dedication of this statue or image.

Therefore, all of his officials came to the dedication and stood before it. Daniel 3:4–6 says, "And the herald proclaimed aloud, "You are commanded, O peoples, nations, and languages, that when you hear the sound of the horn, pipe, lyre, trigon, harp, bagpipe, and every kind of music, you are to fall down and worship the golden image that King Nebuchadnezzar has set up. And whoever does not fall down and worship shall immediately be cast into a burning fiery furnace."

It was now law, and all who lived under Babylonia rule were required to obey the King's decree. To not do so meant death no matter who you were.

The king had placed three Jews over the affairs of the Babylonian provinces. After time, some astrologers came before the king and accused them of refusing to worship the gold image when the music played and refusing to serve or acknowledge King Nebuchadnezzar's gods.

The king became infuriated and filled with rage. He demanded these three heretics be bought before him. So, Shadrach, Meshach, and Abednego were hurried into his presence.

The king then began to question them as to why they refused to obey his decree. Why didn't they worship as he had put into law for all of Babylon?

He decided to give them a shot at redeeming themselves by giving them the choice of falling to their knees and worshiping the idol when they heard the music. If not, immediate judgment would come, and they would be thrown into a blazing furnace.

To add insult to injury, he declared to them, "What god will be able to rescue you from my hand?"

Here is what the three men replied with a holy zeal and confidence:

> *King Nebuchadnezzar, we do not need to defend ourselves before you in this matter. If we are thrown into the blazing furnace, the God we serve is able to deliver us from it, and he will deliver us from Your Majesty's hand. But even if he does not, we want you to know, Your Majesty, that we will not serve your gods or worship the image of gold you have set up* (Daniel 3:16–18).

This enraged the king so much that his attitude became more violent toward them. He ordered the furnace to be heated seven times hotter than usual and commanded the strongest soldiers in his army to tie up the three men and throw them into the furnace. So, these men, wearing their robes, trousers, turbans, and other clothes, were bound and thrown into the furnace.

The king's command was so urgent and the furnace so hot that the flames of the fire killed the soldiers who threw in Shadrach, Meshach, and Abednego. They, being firmly tied, fell right into the blazing furnace.

Then suddenly, the king leaps to his feet in amazement and asks his advisors, "Did we not throw just three men into the blazing furnace?"

They replied, "Certainly, we did, O King."

He shouted, "Look! I see four men walking around in the fire, unbound and unharmed, and the fourth looks like a son of the gods."

Nebuchadnezzar then approached the opening of the blazing furnace from a safe distance and shouted out to Shadrach, Meshach, and Abednego, "Servants of the Most High God, come out and come here."

The three men stepped out of the furnace of fire and all of the king's officials gathered around them. Not only did they see that they were unharmed, but they also realized that they didn't even have the smell of smoke or fire on them or their clothes.

This miracle caused the king to say, "… Blessed be the God of Shadrach, Meshach and Abednego, who hath sent his angel, and delivered his servants that they trusted in him, and have changed the king's word, and yielded their bodies, that they might not serve nor worship any god, except their own God. Therefore, I make a decree, That every people, nation and language, which speak any thing amiss against the God of Shadrach, Meshach, and Abednego, shall be cut in pieces, and their houses shall be a dunghill: because there is no other God that can deliver after this sort" (Daniel 3:28–29).

Then the king proceeded to promote these men unto higher positions in the province of Babylon. This event changed him forever. If you read the full story in the Book of Daniel, you'll find that the king gave a testimony to the power of God:

> *... To the nations and peoples of every language, who live in all the earth: May you prosper greatly! It is my pleasure to tell you about the miraculous signs and wonders that the Most High God has performed for me. How great are his signs, how mighty his wonders! His kingdom is an eternal kingdom; his dominion endures from generation to generation. ... the Most High is sovereign over the kingdoms on earth and gives them to anyone he wishes and sets over them the lowliest of men* (Daniel 4:1–3, 17).

There is so much hope that we can take from this story. It attests to the power of faith in God if we live our lives trusting in Him to deliver us and if we stand up for what we believe. These men did just that under the threat of death.

That furnace was hot. Flesh burns between one hundred forty and one hundred fifty degrees, but the king ordered it to be seven times hotter. What was the result? The three strong men who threw in Shadrach, Meshach, and Abednego died immediately just for tossing them into the oven. Flesh will ignite at temperatures of fourteen hundred and eighteen hundred degrees. These men were literally partially cremated alive.

Can you imagine the fear that these young Jewish men of God must have had when they saw this furnace? Regardless, they told the king, "... Our God whom we serve is able to save us. ... But even if he doesn't, we want to make it clear to you, Your Majesty, that we will never serve your gods or worship the gold statute you have set up" (Daniel 3:17–18).

I am truly inspired by the stance these three took. They refused to obey the laws of the king and instead trusted in God and His Word.

Why is it so hard for the Church and believers to have the same level of faith? Don't we believe anymore in the God of the Bible? Has He died to us?

We can be a people who proclaim, "Our God who we serve is able to save us. We will no longer stand for your political correctness. We will no longer stand for your opposition to God in the classroom and in prayer. We will no longer stand for you killing the unborn. We will no longer stand for you robbing us of our rights. We will no longer stand for your destruction of the family by promoting laws that violate the Bible. We will no longer stand for the removal of God's commandments from our libraries and courtrooms. We will no longer stand for the removal of the cross from anything considered public property.

"We are a Christian nation, and yet if we go through the fire, we will trust Him."

Look, the bottom line is that history proves that when any nation turns its back on God, it dooms itself to destruction. We are and always will be a Christian nation, and even if America falls, it will rise again. It might have to go through the furnace of adversity to get there, though.

God's tender mercy and love is trying to lead us back to a loving relationship with Him. Yes, there will always be those who will oppose us and oppose God, but if we repent and turn back, He will save and restore us back unto Himself.

Why not trust the God of the Old Testament, the God of Shadrach, Meshach, and Abednego?

"So then faith comes by hearing, and by hearing the word of God" (Romans 10:17).

CHAPTER 8

Unity: The Road to Change

Where do we start, and how do we recover?

It begins with each and every one of us falling on our knees, asking God to forgive us for our sins, and turning away from this do-nothing attitude. We're in the here and now of the end-time prophetic clock. God has us in this generation for such a time as this.

We can make a difference if we just turn back to the God of the Bible and quit living this eat-drink-and-be-merry Christianity.

Jesus asked a question, a question that's relevant for today: "… when the son of man cometh, shall he find faith on earth" (Luke 18:8)?

It only takes one man and one voice to get out the message, but what will we do with the message we receive? People, God has not changed. Just because people change and religion changes doesn't mean you can change God or His Word. It just doesn't happen. Go back and reread the Book of Revelation in the New Testament. Is that not an Old Testament message for the last generation which He promised would come?

He is the same yesterday, today, and forever. If you can get that into your heart, it could be the catalyst that might inspire a holy reverence to get back to God.

Jesus Christ is God's Son. He can only do what the Father permits. In Matthew 24, Jesus said that He didn't know the day of His return. That was information that the Father kept to Himself. Only the Father knows the exact period. Furthermore, He made it clear that He only does what He sees the Father do.

Does your son or daughter call you mother or father? Doesn't this mean they're under subjection to you at all times? Occasionally, they emulate what they see you do.

Jesus is our mediator, and He emulates what He sees the Father do. He teaches us to be a mediator for our own children through divine example. He was the Lamb of sacrifice that God poured His wrath onto so that He could redeem all men back unto Himself. He is the only way we have access to God; there is no other path.

I'm not trying to say that He's not one with God. I'm trying to get you to see that no matter what you've been taught or what you've been led to believe, God didn't change the way He deals with the affairs of men and how He judges them just because of what Jesus did.

Jesus was the right arm of God's salvation. Christ was His complete love and mercy through a supreme sacrifice. If anything, what Christ did should give us a more holy reverence and respect for God's wrath. If God didn't spare His own Son, how can we be spared? Did Jesus' sacrifice spare us from the wrath that He said would come in the last days when He gave the revelation to John? Did the apostles not teach that the wrath of God would be poured out in the last days? Sounds like an Old Testament God to me.

Why believe the lie that God has changed and that as a result, we'll all be okay? Now understand this. Believers are protected from God's wrath directly, those who have accepted Jesus Christ as Lord and Savior. Nevertheless, believers are not promised to be protected from man's wrath or from God's judgment of a people or nation who walk in rebellion and refuse to obey His laws.

The scriptures have numerous stories showing that when God judged a nation, He made a way for those who served Him to survive and even thrive if they were taken into captivity. If we really want change, we have to repent and seek God's face with the same unity and love for one another that the believers did when the Church was conceived. We need to do away with all of these counterfeit revivals sweeping through the country and have a real move of God's Spirit. We need to get back to the basics, folks. We need this New Testament gospel preached in an Old Testament way with real signs and wonders and not all of the circus acts I've previously mentioned.

What was the promise that God gave us concerning the last days?

> *In the last days, God says, I will pour out my Spirit on all people. Your sons and daughters will prophecy, your young men will see visions, your old men will dream dreams. Even on my servants, both men and women, I will pour out my Spirit in those days, and they will prophesy. I will show wonders in the heaven above and signs on the earth below … (Acts 2:17–19).*

Jesus Christ gave us this promise, that we could have power and the authority over hell if we have faith in God:

> *I tell you the truth, whatever you forbid on earth will be forbidden in heaven, and whatsoever you permit on earth will be permitted in heaven. Again, truly I tell you that if two of you on earth agree about anything you ask for, it will be done for you by my Father in heaven. For where two or three gather in my name, there am I with them* (Matthew 18:18–20).

Do you understand what Jesus just promised us? He said that His Father, the God of the Old Testament, would act on our behalf if we could come into an agreement on anything. The God of Abraham, Isaac, and Jacob would make it happen if we come to Him through Christ. We have the power in heaven and on earth to bind and loose anything according to Matthew 18.

Most prosperity preachers use these verses to loosen some money from your wallet, and that's the only context in which they like to use it. One of the deceptions they like to use is planting your seed into their ministry. That, to them, is how you are to display faith.

We need to start realizing the potential we have in God and start using the authority He gave us to take back our nation for Him. We, the body of Christ, need to unite, repent, and start binding the forces of darkness that are destroying our country and take back this nation for our God. The legacy of our forefathers and their faith demands we act now.

The believer is the only hope for America. We need a revival of unity, a hunger for the Word of a living God who we believe is the same yesterday, today, and forever. Our faith is the key that will open the windows of heaven, and the Father expects us to obey His Word. We have the power, the authority, the spirit, and the God of Shadrach, Meshach, and Abednego.

Jesus said, "… I tell you the truth, if you had faith even as small as a mustard seed, you could say to this mountain, 'Move from here to there,' and it will move. …" (Matthew 17:20).

NOTHING WILL BE IMPOSSIBLE FOR YOU! Jesus preached the God of the Old Testament here, folks. Sounds like Old Testament to me. Mountain-moving faith is the faith that helped Noah build the ark, and it was what fed and watered six million Jews who left Egypt.

It was that same faith that slew giants, parted oceans, raised the dead, closed the mouths of lions, and caused the blind to see and the deaf to here. Where is that faith now? Why do we as believers not have that same zeal and desire to act upon what God has given us so freely?

> Now faith is the substance of things hoped for and certain of what we do not see. This is what the ancients were commended for (Hebrews 11:1–2).

Do you understand that these men had this faith before the Son of God even came? Still, they believed God and His promises and looked forward to the day when He would come.

Here we are two thousand years into Christ's first coming, and the only faith we can seem to muster is a "plant-your-seed" faith and a "God-will-bless-you" mindset.

And without faith it is impossible to please God, because anyone who comes to him must believe that he exists and that he rewards those who earnestly seek him (Hebrews 11:6).

We have to get our house in order. If the Church won't do it, if the pastor won't do it, and if your religion won't do it, then we must start with ourselves and unify with those of the same faith. In the past, God has used men of faith to change the course of nations. He's more than willing to show love and mercy because His Word gives us the promise of restoration if we repent and seek His face.

God wants to raise a new army of believers, believers who will stand up to injustice and shout the war cry of repentance. He wants believers who have the faith to get out of their comfort zone and fight for what His Word signifies. How can we expect to rule and reign with Him if we can't even control our own leaders in this country now? We let them violate the core principles of our Constitution, which is the written law of the land. We sit by and watch as we self-destruct.

Would you have spoken up if you were there when Pilate asked, "What should I to do with Jesus ..." (Matthew 27:22)? and "... I can find no fault in this man" (Luke 23:4)?

Where are the watchmen, those who follow God? Why do they not protest the satanic insanity that the nation has taken in the last fifty years?

This plant-your-seed faith we feed upon has become more popular than following God's clear voice in scripture. It's like a nightmare to me. The question we have to ask ourselves as believers here is whether God is just as real to us as Christians as He was to Old Testament believers?

So, I began to inquire for myself, *Is this the God in who the prophets believed?*

Let me set the scene for you. When I was first introduced to this phony faith and fanaticism, I almost walked away from God. The pastor had just preached a message that so incited his congregation that people ran around the church sanctuary screaming. They began rolling on the floor, laughing and crying. Some just laid there as if they were under a spell. Some spoke in tongues, and everyone was of the opinion that this was a move of God, "a revival," they said.

I watched as the pastor called people up to the front so that he could deliver some of them from demons. As he began to pray for them through the laying on of hands, I began to witness what I know was just sheer deception and stupidity. They began to spit at others in the church or kick and growl like animals.

It sickened me to see people duped into such fanatical behavior. These people claimed to be Christians, but yet they were fooled into believing they could have demons in them. *What a total farce*, I thought. *Can these people really be this ignorant?*

I mean, how can you speak in tongues one minute and then spit or vomit up demons the next and call it a move of God? Is this what has become of the Church of Jesus Christ? We have to fabricate a false supernatural because our faith is so dead we have to entertain the people to keep them interested. It's so sad and pathetic that we actually call this a revival. The irony of it all is that we judge other religions as false because they don't believe these things.

I thought, *I would never ever want to be part of this freak show.*

Therefore, I walked away from the ministry and pursued business instead. If this was God's power, I wanted nothing to do with it. However, the hunger to know God wouldn't die, so I began to spend countless hours studying the Bible and searching for truth. I even attended Bible College and received my Bachelor of Arts in Biblical Studies all while running a successful business and raising two wonderful sons.

My studies introduced me to the God of heaven, not just to the New Testament God of love, mercy, and grace. I learned He was also the Old Testament God of faith, power, and vengeance.

As I immersed myself in God's Word, I began to realize that this was the Laodicea Age, and people were not really concerned about preaching truth. They were more interested in teaching a health, wealth, and prosperity message, a positive sermon to keep bringing in the people.

The God of the Old Testament was dead to them, and they no longer wanted to hear the truth. They wanted to be comforted in their mediocrity.

Not all believers were the same, and some stayed the course. These believers were the real watchmen, but as goes the way of all true men of God, they were labeled crazies for their outlandish teachings of repentance and judgment. The Spirit of God led the fire-and-brimstone preachers to warn impending financial judgment if America continued on this course of rebellion. Now the warnings of these watchmen have been fulfilled just in the last few years.

There is no unity in the body. False teachings and religious lies have destroyed real faith in God.

People have been victimized by false prophets who only teach what will bring in the fattest offering. Every religious organization in the United States has been affected in some way by scandal, whether it's financial or sexual. It destroys the people's faith in God and man. The only remedy, the only real cure for this sickness of faith, is for believers to repent and leave the churches that preached these lies. Then they need to unify under the banner of the written Word of God.

The Holy Spirit is a gentleman. He will not or cannot bring shame to the Kingdom of God. Don't let these profit peddlers tell you otherwise.

For such people are false apostles, deceitful workers, masquerading as apostles of Christ. And no wonder for Satan himself masquerades as an angel of light. It is not surprising, then, if his servants also masquerade as servants of righteousness. Their end will be what their actions deserve (2 Corinthians 11:13–15).

Paul gave believers an itinerary of disciplines for orderly worship that must be adhered to if we are to win others to faith in Christ. These disciplines can be found in 1Corininthians. They are put in place for the unification of believers so that we might display the glory of God both through words and through our acts of worship.

The discipline that the Church seems to be lacking, especially in charismatic circles, is the doctrine of the Holy Spirit. For some reason they seem to think that God's Holy Spirit will cause people to roll around on the floor like they're having a epileptic seizure or laugh uncontrollably or even shout out in some unknown tongue and call it a move of God.

Paul wrote in 1Corinthians 14,

> *Now brothers and sisters, if I come to you and speak in tongues, what good will I be to you, unless I bring you some revelation or knowledge or prophecy or word of instruction? ... Unless you speak intelligible words with your tongue, how will anyone know what you are saying ...* (1 Corinthians 14:6, 9).

If the Holy Spirit is going to speak, Paul is saying it will bring us revelation, knowledge, prophecy, or instruction through an intelligible language so that all can understand. It will unify the body of Christ, not cause confusion and reckless behavior. He made it perfectly clear that if some who don't understand or some unbelievers who come into the church and see these things, will they not say you are out of your mind?

How is it so easy for believers to be deceived into thinking this type of behavior would bring anyone back to their church? Do they have any idea as to how ridiculous we look to the world?

Paul said that a true move of God takes place when God reveals the secrets of men's hearts so that they'll be led to repent and turn to Him. As a result, that person will fall down and proclaim, "God is really among you."

Nowhere in the scriptures is there a mention of the things we see in some congregations today. They live in discord over the silliest of doctrines that were perpetuated by religious puritans believing they had heard from God.

The congregation of the saints should be a place of reverent worship to God, not a place where people run around the church, laughing uncontrollably, and rolling around on the floor speaking in tongues like babbling babies. It's not a place where miracles are determined and validated by falling backward into the waiting arms of catchers or having someone prophesying lies of wealth and prosperity over you because you have given to their ministry.

The Church is to be a place of holiness, a place of worship, a place of repentance, a place where real miracles take place without begging for money. It's a place where lives are touched, and people are changed. It has to be a place of learning obedience to God's Word.

You are part of a spiritual family called and separated to live a life that honors your Lord. How has it come to this apostasy? Why have we torn ourselves from the body of Christ and created such disunity amongst ourselves.

We have allowed the doctrines of demons to influence our teaching about the validity of the Bible and adhered to religious influences that are completely contrary to what the scripture says. What a mastermind Satan is. He has tried for over two thousand years to confuse and confound believers with religious lies. In the end and through God's goodness and grace, the Holy Spirit sends us real men of God to lead us back through repentance. We are all one body with many gifts. The only way the body works is in unison, whether physically or spiritually. Should we not take the greatest opportunity in human history to impact our generation with the truth of God's Word?

Paul said in 1 Corinthians 2:6–7,

We do, however, speak a message of wisdom among the mature, but not the wisdom of this age or of the rulers of this age, who are coming to nothing. No, we declare God's wisdom, a mystery that has been hidden and that God destined for our glory before time began.

Is this not the age that the prophets and apostles anticipated? Are we to squander the gifts that God has given us on the doctrines of devils and so-called moves of God? These dog-and-pony shows are nothing more than magic performances that attempt to liberate you from your hard-earned money.

God's Kingdom is not a matter of talk but of power. The Holy Spirit did not come to embarrass the Kingdom of God and make us look like fools. He came to teach us, guide us, and show us things to come.

Our bodies are temples in which the Spirit of God lives once we accept Christ into our lives. Can you fathom what I'm saying? The Spirit of the living God of creation dwells in us. It's beyond me how in the world these religious sons of deception can accuse the Holy Spirit of making us act and look like crazy fanatics when we gather for a revival. It's an emotional, irrational flesh-show church, not a revival. This type of behavior has led to a spiritual death because most believers see these types of actions as a move of God. To them, this is all they need.

The Holy Spirit is the third person of the Godhead. He works in every dimension. Through the Spirit, God created and preserves all things, visible or invisible, that are created.

Divine attributes describe the Holy Spirit: eternal, omnipresent (always present), omnipotent (all powerful), and omniscient (all knowing). He was present at creation and is actively involved in regeneration. He's also the catalyst for resurrection. The Bible says He is equal to God, the Father, and the Son.

The Spirit is described as a person because He exercises the attributes of a personality. He has a will and feelings. He teaches, witnesses, intercedes, speaks, commands, and testifies. He may be grieved, lied to, and blasphemed.

Now do you think with all these divine attributes He would cause such confusion in the Church and then cause people to act in such a way as to bring reproach upon the Kingdom of God? Are there any eyewitness accounts of Jesus or His followers doing some of the things we see now in some charismatic circles? Nope.

The Lord said He would not leave us as orphans, but He would send the Comforter, one is like unto Himself to assist us in our walk in this life. How, then, are the crowds manipulated into believing that all of these crazy occurrences we see in churches are real if He sent One like unto Himself? No wonder we're treated with such scorn.

The Churches have no real power except for that which it has created for our weak-minded congregations through our deceptive teachings. He didn't send this spirit that's prevalent in today's churches. Satan did. Why? He wanted to cause confusion and separate us from the truth of God's Word, which destroys the works of Satan. He can't allow believers to wield that sword. What better way to deceive the masses than to introduce man-made religious doctrines based on private interpretations.

Most people don't read and study their Bible. They just go to church and take what the pastor says as the written Word of God, so many truths are missed. As I mentioned before, we force ourselves into bondage through beliefs and teachings within organizations that don't even line up with the scriptures.

If only every pastor in America could get together and agree with one another and forget themselves. If only they could proclaim, "Let's break down the barriers and disregard our differences and seek a common goal. Let's proclaim a fast and a call to repentance. Let's unify to seek God's face to forgive our iniquity and the iniquity of our nation."

We could save our nation. The only way revival will come is if we acknowledge we're at fault and trust in the mercy of God's tender-loving grace to restore us back to what our ancestors fought and died for years ago.

The Church should be a place of miracles, a place where people can be healed from their sickness through the power that Christ commissioned to us. The blind should see, the crippled made to walk, the deaf to hear, lives restored, hearts changed, and yes, even the dead raised. Impossible, you say. Yes, it is for a dead, faithless church.

I can't believe what has happened with this blatant apostasy. Just like when Jesus went into the temple in Jerusalem and cried out, "… It is written, 'My house shall be called a house of prayer, but you are making it a den of robbers'" (Matthew 21:13).

At present, the same remains true. The Temple or Church has become a place of collection and not a place of redemption. The blind do not see. The deaf do not hear, and the lame do not walk. It's time to get back to the Old Testament God. If our churches won't embrace this God, then we as believers must.

Men like Martin Luther had enough of the lies and religion taught by Catholicism. He decided that obeying God was better than obeying man. So in 1517, he posted his ninety-five theses on Catholic Church doors for all to read. This act of defiance resulted in his excommunication by the pope and his condemnation as an outlaw by the emperor.

His theology challenged the authority of the Church and the pope. He taught that the Bible is the only source of divinely revealed knowledge. Because of his desire for people to know the truth of God's Word, he stood up for what he believed to be true. That is, he openly proclaimed the Bible as the final authority, not what religion teaches or governments allow.

We need this tenacity and commitment. We need to call our pastors out on their disregard of the truth. We need to demand that the walls of division be torn down and this useless bickering over doctrines be stopped. We need to get back to the basics, and that starts with each and every one of us repenting and living what we believe.

Let's quit begging for money and stop perpetrating the plant-your-seed kind of faith. It's spiritual dung. Let's take up our lamps and ask God to fill them with the oil of His Spirit and do the exploits that Jesus said we have the ability to do through faith in His Name.

These circus acts we see on television and in our churches are a disgrace to why the apostles laid down their lives. How can we claim we'll die for Christ when we won't even die to the world? How can we claim we have faith when we have no works for the world to see?

You want proof? Then tell me when was the last time you saw a blind man see again? When did you witness a crippled man walk, a deaf person hear, or the dead come back to life? Should not the Church of Jesus Christ be the most powerful place of worship on the face of the earth?

Paul said, "Faith without works is dead" (James 2:14–26).

I'm not talking about this seed-faith garbage. I'm talking about the faith that will cause us to stand up against the injustice of our government the way Moses stood up to Pharaoh. I'm talking about the kind of faith that Daniel showed when he prayed three times a day in Babylon even when he knew it was a crime against the current governmental authority. I'm talking about a revolutionary kind of faith, a faith to believe that God will be with us when we take a stand for what is right and just.

We need to live as if we believe the Bible is true and not like the Bible is a great historical record about a time gone by. God has not changed. He is the same yesterday, today, and forever. It's time for the saints of the Most-High God to shake off this fear of government and speak out on what we believe is true.

We need to unify under the banner of repentance. No more divisions. Stick to the core principles of the Holy scriptures that say, "… Love one another. As I have loved you …" (John 13: 34).

A real move of God and revival will occur when every believer decides he wants a new beginning of obedience to God. A revival is nothing less than a conviction of sin on the part of believers and the Church. It doesn't come by raising money or glorified flesh shows. A true revival brings about a search of the hidden sins of the heart and causes conviction for those sins. We need to see these sins in such a light that we find it impossible to maintain God's acceptance because of our sin.

It's time we allow the love of God to be renewed in our hearts. We need to see ourselves as sinners in desperate need of His mercy and love. We have to throw down our pride and submit to His will for our lives. It is a grace awakening, a reformation of saints and sinners alike. It has to begin with the Church first, the saints second, and the sinners third. A revival within the Church is the only possible way to wash away our reproach and restore dignity back unto the saints of God.

We must have an Old Testament move of God to regain any credibility to the world. Our own sin has caused such a disgrace to the testimony of the gospel. Unless revival comes, we will face God's judgment for sin. The facts are that Christians are more to blame. The sinners can't be converted if there's no God, and if there's no God, to whom will they be accountable? How can we convince them that God is real if we live like there is no God?

Look, I'm just as guilty as the next man. It starts with the man in the mirror first. With that being said, what will you do? It's your responsibility to work out your own salvation with fear and trembling. Let the revival start in your heart, and let the change begin right there in you and with your family and your church through the power of your testimony.

The world as we know it is changing more rapidly every day. With that change, a strong disconnection with Christianity occurs because of the personal trash the Church has laid bare to the world over the last fifty or so years. We've brought such a reproach upon Christianity that we have lost any influence we might have had.

It's time for the saints of God within each religious body to call the Church out on its failure to follow the Holy Word. It's time for the saints to take on the spirit of Martin Luther and destroy the works of the devil that has caused such disunity among the Church body. It's time for a new body of believers to break the chains of religious bondage and get back to the faith of the prophets and apostles. Why not, saints? We've been given the power and the authority. It's time we begin to recognize our power is not delegated to raising money every chance we get. Instead, it's delegated to show that the power of God is just as real today as it was two thousand years ago when the Church was born.

Meet with God yourself. He lives in your heart. Your body is His temple. Let's repent of our worldly attitude and our rebellious ingratitude. We have lived in unbelief for so long that we have forgotten how to pray with feeling.

Where is the same love for one another that He has shown us? Jesus is coming back. Do you want to make a difference in this life, or is it always going to have to be about you? We have been given the gift of eternal life if we walk in obedience to God. It's an obedience that comes through faith in His Name.

How long before revival is up to us. It can come now or never. I want to touch as many lives as possible with the truth of God's Word. Does not the Bible teach us that we have been given authority over all of the power of the enemy?

It's time to make a change for our own salvation. We can no longer allow this hate and disunity to control our churches and our lives. We must get back to the truth of God's Word and stand our ground against these wicked men in our churches and government.

It's time for a twenty-first-century reformation, and it can only start with us.

CHAPTER 9

The Power of Grace

Grace, grace, a lifetime of grace, saved from my sin and my own disgrace. Freed from a lifetime of sin. Cleansed from the darkness that was born within. The power of His blood has set me free. It was grace that saved a wretch like me.

There are times when I look back over my life and just don't understand how God could love a worthless sinner like me. I live in the shame of my past. It's a thorn in my mind, a rebuke to my soul, and it haunts me when I lie down to sleep.

No matter how you try to compromise with sin, it will bite back with deadly accuracy and precision. You eventually reap what you sow. It might take weeks, months, or years, but it will find you. When it does, it will sift you, rebuke you, and rob you of any sense of security you might think you have in this life.

Proverbs 14:12 tells us that "There is a way that seems right to a man, but its end is death."

Sin seems so attractive at the time. Its passion is relentless. It teases us with pleasure. It caresses us with foreplay, and it makes love to our minds. It soothes us into believing it's okay. Surely God will understand. It causes our hearts to flutter with anticipation and excitement, and we become numb to the truth. We put aside the voice of reason, and we slide into the bed of death and destruction. Drugs, alcohol, lying, cheating, stealing, lust, adultery, sexual immorality, hate, perversion, witchcraft, murder, violence, hypocrisy, gossip, and compromise are all just waiting to lure you into its den of desire and deceit.

Paul wrote of his own battle with sin in Romans 7:18–20:

> *For I know that nothing good lives in me, that is, in my sinful nature. For I have the desire to do what is good, but I cannot carry it out. For I do not the good I want to do, but the evil I do not want to do—this I keep on doing. Now if I do what I do not want to do, it is no longer I who do it, but it is sin living in me that does it.*

Every one of us fights this same battle with sin. At times we know the right thing to do, but we just can't seem to walk away from its enticement and pleasure. We become trapped by our own desires, and we lose focus of who we are in Christ before stumbling into the pit of failure. It's part of the human condition, a continuous and repetitive act of disobedience. It's what we do when we stumble that affects us and our relationship with God. Do we confess our sin as scripture requires, or do we just act as if it never happened and keep living as if God didn't see it?

In II Samuel 12, David did the latter even though He was a man after God's own heart. The giant killer acted like God didn't see his sin of adultery; therefore, no confession of his offense came forth until Nathan, the Lord's prophet, called him out on it almost a year after the fact. David showed contempt for the Lord by being so dishonest, and it caused the Lord's enemies to show contempt also. David's sin had found him out, and God had to act. Justice had to be served because David did not repent until his sin was exposed.

David said to Nathan, "I have sinned against the Lord. ..." (II Samuel 12:13).

Who knows? He might have never repented if God's grace had not sent Nathan to rebuke him for his sin. This grace leads us to repentance, especially when we willfully sin like David did.

Paul wrote in Romans 2:4, "Or do you show contempt for the riches of his kindness, forbearance and patience, not realizing that God's kindness is intended to lead you to repentance?"

God's great patience and love draws us to a place of repentance, a place of reconciliation for our failures, and a place of pure peace. That's why where sin abounds, grace abounds even more (Romans 5:20).

When God allowed His Son to leave the glories of heaven and come to this earth to die for the sins of the whole world, He displayed the riches of His eternal grace and love. In Him, we have redemption through His blood, the forgiveness of sin, and it all came by grace. Nevertheless, unfortunately some of us use that grace as a license to sin, a free pass to do whatever we want. We think that come Sunday, we can just go to church and seek a superficial repentance that doesn't come from the heart.

The problem is that if we keep sinning and think we can depend on God's grace to save us, God's grace doesn't apply. We have not sought true repentance; we have sought a repentance of comfort for the guilt we feel for being disobedient to God.

If you die to sin, how can you keep living in sin? The scriptures make it perfectly clear that we are not to let sin reign in our mortal bodies. If we do, sin becomes a master over us, and we give into its desires to defy God's law. We're no longer under the law of sin if we walk in God's grace. This grace teaches us not to sin but to obey so that we don't keep sinning.

I lived in Mississippi for about seven years. Coming from South Florida, I wasn't too familiar with Mardi Gras. From what I've seen and learned while living there was that it's a big event and is based on the practice of carnival celebrations. It lasts for about a month and ends on Fat Tuesday, the day before Ash Wednesday. This is when Lent begins, a forty-day period of fasting and repentance, but Sundays aren't included during this time.

The common theme in Mardi Gras is to party hard, to eat, drink, and be merry, and to show no inhibitions. It's not uncommon during this celebration to see public nudity, drunkenness, debauchery, sexual acts, and violence.

Believe it or not, but most who attend this event think they can do all the sinning they want because when Lent arrives, they can just repent and repeat the same behavior again next year. Herein lays the problem, especially for those of us who claim to be Christians. Proverbs 26:11 states, "As a dog returns to his vomit, so fools repeat their folly."

Let me make this a little more descriptive to prove a point. Have you ever watched a dog eat? A dog never gets enough.

It'll keep eating no matter what you throw at it. Sometimes there's no chewing, especially if other dogs are around. It'll just swallow the food and keep eating, wanting more and more until finally it vomits.

Then up comes the food, stomach bile, and a river of salvia and snot. Sounds scrumptious right? (Yuck!)

What does the dog do after this disgusting act of gluttony? It walks right back over and starts eating what it just vomited, lapping up every bit of it like it had never eaten. It continues going back for more, repeating the same process every chance it gets so that it can keep its belly full, totally oblivious to the fact there is no more room in its stomach.

God gave us this illustration to prove a valid point that only a fool would return to his sinful ways after God's grace had led him to true repentance. Only a fool would keep repeating the same offense over and over again with the ideology that God will just forgive anyway. Why not just keep sinning and use His grace as a permit to do whatever we want? We want no accountability. This is not true repentance. It's blasphemy to think we can sin with the mindset of seeking repentance at a later time when we conveniently feel convicted.

We need to learn to operate in the grace that leads us to walk in obedience, not the grace that allows us to walk in repetitive sin. Unfortunately in some churches, a false doctrine exists. This religious falsehood says you can become absolved of your sin by confessing to a priest or by acts of works, whether it's rubbing beads, repeating the same prayer, marking your forehead with ash, and/or praying to certain saints. Again, this is not true repentance.

Repentance means to turn away from a past action, to feel sorrow for a sin or a fault to the point that one changes his or her life for the better.

Galatians 2:18 says, "If I rebuild what I destroyed, I prove that I am a lawbreaker."

How can we keep making the same confession for the same sin over and over again? How can we expect to walk in victory over that sin when we keep repeating it with the sole intent of using God's grace as a license to keep sinning?

You're rebuilding what you asked God to destroy. You've been crucified with Christ. You no longer live under sin, but because of God's grace, you now live in this body as a living testimony of the power of Christ over sin. He has made that same victory over sin available to you through faith in Him.

Christ told Paul in II Corinthians 12:9: "... 'My grace is sufficient for you, for my power is made perfect in weakness. ...'"

God knows our weaknesses. He knows the sins that beset us and distract us from our walk with Him. Each and every one of us has things in us that we have to contend with every day. They're our secret sins that we try to hide out of site from the rest of the world. It's those things that we can't seem to escape from, and they convict us, grief us, and have a grip on our soul. We pray; we cry; and we fight against this desire to sin, but eventually we give into our weakness and do the things we don't want to do. It's our actions after we stumble that either lead us to a grace awakening or a grace killing.

A grace awakening is when we stumble or fail. Afterward, we go to God in true repentance, seeking to be changed and transformed. We seek and ask for a renewed heart and mind to help us overcome the adversity of our plaguing sin or sins. It can take years to gain victory, but as long as you live a life trying to overcome these weaknesses with sincerity of heart, God's grace is in full effect. He sees into the heart of your condition, and He patiently uses His grace, love, and mercy to lead you to the victory that you so desperately want.

A grace killing is just the opposite. In the lust of your flesh, you intentionally sin with the attitude that you can live and do whatever you want because God will forgive you anyway because of His grace. It's treating the sacrifice of Christ and the goodness and love of God with contempt, believing you still have salvation.

In II Peter 2:1–22, Peter responded to this form of apostasy and the religious leaders who teach such open rebellion:

> But there were also false prophets among the people, just as there will be false teachers among you. They will secretly introduce destructive heresies, even denying the sovereign Lord who bought them— bringing swift destruction on themselves. Many will follow their depraved conduct and will bring the way of truth into disrepute.
>
> In their greed these teachers will exploit you with fabricated stories. Their condemnation has long been hanging over them, and their destruction has not been sleeping. For if God did not spare angels when they sinned, but sent them to hell, putting them in chains of darkness to be held for judgment; if he did not spare the ancient world when he brought the flood on its ungodly

people, but protected Noah, a preacher of righteousness, and seven others; if he condemned the cities of Sodom and Gomorrah by burning them to ashes, and made them an example of what is going to happen to the ungodly; and if he rescued Lot, a righteous man, who was distressed by the depraved conduct of the lawless (for that righteous man, living among them day after day, was tormented in his righteous soul by the lawless deeds he saw and heard)—if this is so, then the Lord knows how to rescue the godly from trials and to hold the unrighteous for punishment on the day of judgment. This is especially true of those who follow the corrupt desire of the flesh and despise authority.

Bold and arrogant, they are not afraid to heap abuse on celestial beings; yet even angels, although they are stronger and more powerful, do not heap abuse on such beings when bringing judgment on them from the Lord. But these people blaspheme in matters they do not understand. They are like unreasoning animals, creatures of instinct, born only to be caught and destroyed, and like animals, they too will perish.

They will be paid back with harm for the harm they have done. Their idea of pleasure is to carouse in broad daylight. They are blots and blemishes, reveling in their pleasures while they feast with you. With eyes full of adultery, they never stop sinning; they seduce the unstable; they are experts in greed—an accursed brood! They have left the straight way and wandered off to follow the way of Balaam son of Bezer, who loved the wages of wickedness. But he was rebuked for his wrongdoing by a donkey—an animal without speech—

who spoke with a human voice and restrained the prophet's madness. These people are springs without water and mists driven by a storm. Blackest darkness is reserved for them.

For they mouth empty, boastful words and, by appealing to the lustful desires of the flesh, they entice people who are just escaping from those who live in error. They promise them freedom, while they themselves are slaves of depravity—for "people are slaves to whatever has mastered them." If they have escaped the corruption of the world by knowing our Lord and Savior Jesus Christ and are again entangled in it and are overcome, they are worse off at the end than they were at the beginning.

It would have been better for them not to have known the way of righteousness, than to have known it and then to turn their backs on the sacred command that was passed on to them. Of them the proverbs are true: "A dog returns to its vomit," and, "A sow that is washed returns to her wallowing in the mud.

Peter was well-aware of the depths of God's grace. He had sat at the Lord's feet, receiving God's Word from the mouth of His Creator. He witnessed the life-changing power of grace. He saw it change hearts. He saw it heal the sick. He watched as it brought the dead back to life again and was there to be a living testimony of its power over sin.

Yet even though Peter had sat and heard every message from the Lord and seen and experienced every miracle when times got tough, he denied he even knew Him. Now some might think what Peter had done was unforgivable, but this gave God the chance to show the riches of the grace He was showing the world. He forgives the unforgivable.

After Christ's resurrection, some of the women who followed Jesus were on their way to the tomb to anoint the body of the Lord. They assumed Jesus was still in that tomb. Before arriving, they became concerned on how they would roll away the stone that blocked and covered the entrance.

Upon arriving, they looked up and saw the stone had already been rolled away. They immediately rushed inside to see an angel sitting where their Lord's body once had lain, and they were startled.

"Don't be alarmed," he said. "You are looking for Jesus of Nazarene, who was crucified. He has risen! ... But go, tell the disciples and Peter, 'He is going ahead of you into Galilee. ...'" (Mark 16:6–7).

The angel had emphasized the importance of notifying Peter separately that the Lord whom He had denied had risen from the dead.

I'm sure that confusion had set into Peter's heart. He probably thought that Christ would conquer the Roman army and restore Israel to its former glory. That's why he took up the sword. But when he realized his assumptions were not to be, he backslid in the face of fear and adversity and denied that he even knew the Lord, not once but three times.

Grace was there, though. It was a grace of restoration and mercy.

In John 21, we see Christ asking Peter three times, "Peter do you love me?"

Peter's response was, "Yes, my Lord. I love you."

Can you see the significance of this testament? Peter

uttered three proclamations of love and then three proclamations of denial. They all came from the lips of the same man who had just experienced the grace of God in action. Even before Peter had denied Christ, he had already been forgiven.

God loves you more than you can understand or comprehend. His Word declares that He doesn't want anyone to perish, no not one. He knows you have weaknesses. He knows of your secret sin. He's aware of your failure, and He also knows it might take some time before you overcome these sins, but He loves you anyway.

His grace means unmerited favor, but it comes with the condition that you repent of sin and walk in the grace He provides to overcome that sin. It's not there so that you can go on sinning but to keep you from sin.

In Titus 2:11–13, Paul wrote, "For the grace of God that bringeth salvation hath appeared to all men, Teaching us that, denying ungodliness and worldly lusts, we should live soberly, righteously, and godly, in this present world; Looking for that blessed hope, and the glorious appearing of the great God and our Savior Jesus Christ;"

Do you see God's intent and purpose in providing grace? It's His ground rules on how to say NO to sin. Grace teaches us not to go on sinning but to live a life that is surrendered to His perfect will, a self-controlled life that is not influenced by the actions of others. Rather, it chooses to say no even if everyone one else says yes.

Grace gives us the ability to become the righteousness of God through our faith in Christ. It leads us daily in our walk with God to a place of intimate fellowship with Him.

In this day and age with the attraction of worldly pleasures that are promoted as tantalizing rights, we need grace.

"Come now, let us reason together, says the LORD: though your sins are like scarlet, they shall be as white as snow; though they are red like crimson, they shall become like wool" (Isaiah 1:18).

Here it is in a nutshell, a simplistic explanation from the Holy scriptures:

> *As for you, you were dead in your transgressions and sins, in which you used to live when you followed the ways of this world and of the ruler of the kingdom of the air, the spirit who is now at work in those who are disobedient. All of us also lived among them at one time, gratifying the cravings of our flesh and following its desires and thoughts. Like the rest, we were by nature deserving of wrath. But because of his great love for us, God, who is rich in mercy, made us alive with Christ even when we were dead in transgressions--it is by grace you have been saved. And God raised us up with Christ and seated us with him in the heavenly realms in Christ Jesus, in order that in the coming ages he might show the incomparable riches of his grace, expressed in his kindness to us in Christ Jesus. For it is by grace you have been saved, through faith--and this is not from yourselves, it is the gift of God--not by works, so that no one can boast. For we are God's handiwork, created in Christ Jesus to do good works, which God prepared in advance for us to do* (Ephesians 2:1–10).

Do you understand how God uses grace? It's His catalyst to lead the heart to a true repentance. It's a free gift given with unconditional merits to save us if we follow the simple plan that God has laid out for all men.

Grace is the treasure of heaven. It provides redemption to the worst of sinners through a pure repentant heart. It calls out to all men and women everywhere. It's underserved, and it's free.

If you've been using the grace of God as a license to sin, I encourage you to repent and seek His face. God loves you enough to forgive every sin you have committed past, present, and in the future.

His love calls out to you to repent so that you can be saved. God desires for all to come to the knowledge of this truth. There's no truth but what the Holy Word declares as truth. The truth to which we testify is that we are to serve Him as slaves freed from the power of sin.

We've been bought with a price that can never be repaid. It's underserved, unmerited, and it can't be earned through acts of righteousness. It's free and available to all, and it's just a prayer away.

Find it today, and it will change your life forever.

Grace, grace, a lifetime of grace, saved from my sin and my own disgrace. Freed from a lifetime of sin. Cleansed from the darkness that was born within. The power of His blood has set me free. It was grace that saved a wretch like me.

CHAPTER 10

A Vision of the Future

We are at the culmination of the greatest event in human history. I'm talking about how ever since God commanded Adam to come forth from the dust of the ground, this generation shall clearly witness the beginning of God's Kingdom becoming the kingdom of this world.

The time is coming when Satan will be bound to the abyss for a thousand years where he can't interfere in the affairs of men. Jesus will set up a theocracy to which all of the nations and governments of the earth will answer. The rule of those governments shall be upon His shoulders.

He shall set up His saints to rule and reign over the kingdoms of this earth. They all shall be under subjection to Him and shall rule based on His Lordship. He shall restore Earth to its original creative state, and He shall do away with the curse that had befallen upon this world because of man's sin. He shall do away with the need for men to learn war because God will bring swift justice for any act of rebellion against the authority of His government.

Those who live and survive at the second coming after the battle of Armageddon will go on to live into the thousand-year reign of Christ. They will be required to submit to His sovereignty and His rule. No exceptions. Free will in government is gone, and He shall rule with an iron rod. Peace will be our covering and joy our fullness.

God shall wipe away all of our tears, and He shall speak to us face to face. We'll be brought into the fullness of His wisdom and love, and we'll never have to deal with sin again after the thousand-year millennium ends. All of His creation shall live at peace from animal to man. We'll not kill anymore or make war again in His Kingdom.

In 1 Corinthians 2:9 we are told, "However, as it is written: 'What no eye has seen, what no ear has heard, and what no human mind has conceived' -- the things God has prepared for those who love him."

By His Spirit, God has revealed to us the soon fulfillment of end-time events. With that being said, I want you to imagine a world restored back to its creative state, pure, fresh air with no allergens, smog, or pollution. Envision a world where water is clean and clear with no chlorine, fluoride, or chemicals to harm us. Picture lakes and oceans that are abundant in life and free from pollution. Visualize Earth maintaining a perfect temperature and humidity so that all life thrives within the balance of God's order.

I believe that all of the earth will be assimilated into the kingdom of heaven as God works through Jesus Christ to prepare us for eternity during the thousand years of His reign on this planet. Our knowledge will be increased so that we will be able to use one-hundred percent of our brain's capacity, and we will learn the secret things of God.

I also believe we will be able to use thought as a form of travel and be able to move freely in and out of different dimensions. Different worlds will be available to us. We can enjoy the beauty of God's creation at a universal level in our new bodies, traveling anywhere He permits us to go. We can travel and see new galaxies where He's creating new life-forms, or we may possibly be put in charge of watching over these new worlds as stewards to monitor their growth.

All things that were invisible will now be visible to us. We'll see with eternal eyes, not eyes of flesh and blood, and the same is true with all of the senses of the human body.

We'll experience a completely new level of perception of God's true design. Heaven will hold the mansions that God has prepared for us.

We'll be able to move freely from place to place in all of His creation to enjoy everything that He has given us. Our new bodies will be a place of perpetual spiritual worship to Him so that where ever we are in all of His creation, the worship of Him will live within us.

The Bible doesn't say much of anything about what takes place during the thousand years of God's rule. I think that's because there were incomprehensible things to the writers. God knew they wouldn't understand without a detailed explanation, so He decided to keep these things to Himself and for us to experience when the time of fulfillment arrives.

I believe He'll answer all of our questions about all things, and He'll permit us to do all things that our heart desires. I believe He'll allow us to time travel so that we can examine what actually took place during some of the most important events in human history. This will be heaven to us, so God will fill us with the knowledge of

His understanding. We can then understand His justice, love, mercy, and grace throughout the course of man's rule on earth.

Man will be exalted higher than the angels to a place of reverence in His Kingdom. The Bible says in Genesis 3:22, "... The man has now become like one of us, knowing good and evil. ..."

Have you ever realized what these verses are actually saying, starting in Genesis which relate to God's creation of man? Maybe this was part of God's plan from the beginning, to create a being that could walk in equality with God and be His eternal family.

Look at Genesis 1:26–27. "... 'Let us make mankind in our image, in our likeness,' ... So God created mankind in his own image, in the image of God he created them; ..."

We are the mirror image of God, so man alone has this attribute and honor from Him to reflect His image. But even though we were created in His image and likeness, we still didn't have all of the attributes of His knowledge until after the fall.

Genesis 3:22 said, "And the Lord God said, 'The man has now become like one of us, knowing good and evil. He must not be allowed to reach out his hand and take also from the tree of life and eat, and live forever.'"

Notice in these verses that man wasn't merely created in God's image. After the fall, God pronounced that man is now like Him because he has become aware of the knowledge of good and evil. Because man won't live forever, He removed access to the tree of life.

Have you ever stopped to think that maybe this was God's plan from the very beginning? Do you suppose that God set things in motion to make sure that man would fall?

How else could we become completely like God if we didn't have the knowledge of good and evil or right from wrong? It would strip us of our own free will, and we would have just been puppets created in His image without the ability to choose and love freely.

I put this out there for you to discern for yourself. God had a brilliant plan from the very beginning, and I'm sure He knew what would happen in the Garden of Eden when He first thought about us. All things were designed for the intended purpose of creating a life-form that would serve Him through the loyalty of love and not by the loyalty of law.

Lucifer and his angels served God because of their loyalty to the laws put in place in heaven before the creation of all things. They had no choice. It was either serve God or be thrown out of heaven. It's never mentioned once that Lucifer loved God or that he served by his own free will. He rebelled because he thought in the pride of his heart that he could govern creation better than God. He wanted his throne above God's throne. He wanted the worship, the praise, and the glory that belong to God alone. Other angels also joined Lucifer in this war of rebellion against God. They followed him with a clear mission and that mission was to enthrone Lucifer into a place of lordship over heaven and to dethrone God.

We're caught between a war with two powers. Both want absolute sovereignty. The reason is because of God's love. Since God is omnipotent, omniscient, and omnipresent, He could have quashed and destroyed Lucifer as soon as He knew the thoughts and intents of his heart. But He chose not to do so. Why do you think that is?

The Bible says, "You said in your heart, 'I will ascend to the heavens; I will raise my throne above the stars of God; ... I will make myself like the Most High.'" (Isaiah 14:13–14).

God is a loving God who has the power to know His creation's thoughts and intentions. He knew from the beginning of time what the outcome of the rebellion in heaven would produce. He allowed it because he could see down through time and see the trillions of redeemed saints who chose to love and serve him by their own free will.

I don't know about you, but I don't think my spirit was hanging out someplace waiting for God to put me in the middle of a war between Him and Lucifer. He planted me in a body that was cursed before I was born.

As soon as you leave the womb, you're predestined to die. You are sinless but condemned. God's purpose in this is so that men might seek Him and believe the message of His love and grace and come to a personal knowledge of who He is. God has put on full display how light overcomes darkness and good always conquers evil for all of creation to see and witness. I have no other logical explanation that comes to my mind about God's predetermined will. I do know that whatever does take place in God's creation, I'll put my hope in Him. I'll trust in His love, mercy, and grace to guide and direct me into the Kingdom He has prepared for those who love Him by their own free will

I know it's hard to accept that when we're born we are already condemned to sin and suffer death. It's not fair, not just, and surely not right. Who are we to question what God does in His universe? Does not the scripture say, "For my thoughts are not your thoughts, neither are your ways my ways ..." (Isaiah 55:8)

No man wants to tackle questions about the mysteries of God's predestined will, especially a man of the cloth.

They surely won't tell you a truth that puts the blame on God. They feel in their arrogance that they must defend God, but He is God. "… Should the thing that was created say to the one who created it, 'Why have you made me like this?'" (Romans 9:20).

Yes, God is responsible for everything that occurs in His universe. He knew billions of years ago that Lucifer would fall. He allows sin and uses it for His own purpose. You or I can do nothing about that. We have to accept by faith, and we must trust in the power of the written word, the Word that became flesh, the Lord Jesus Christ.

As John 1:1–14 states,

In the beginning was the Word, and the Word was with God, and the Word was God. He was with God in the beginning. Through him all things were made; without him nothing was made that has been made. In him was life, and that life was the light of all mankind. The light shines in the darkness, and the darkness has not overcome it. There was a man sent from God whose name was John. He came as a witness to testify concerning that light, so that through him all might believe. He himself was not the light; he came only as a witness to the light. The true light that gives light to everyone was coming into the world. He was in the world, and though the world was made through him, the world did not recognize him. He came to that which was his own, but his own did not receive him. Yet to all who did receive him, to those who believed in his name, he gave the right to become children of God—children born not of natural descent, nor of human decision or a husband's will, but born of God. The Word became

> *flesh and made his dwelling among us. We have seen his glory, the glory of the one and only Son, who came from the Father, full of grace and truth.*

Yes, God will win. He has let us know the outcome of the war so that we could make the right choice.

Let us examine a passage of scripture in the Book of Job. This section points to some astounding evidence of how God allows evil to happen in order to work out His ultimate purpose.

> *One day the angels came to present themselves before the Lord, and Satan also came with them. The Lord said to Satan, "Where have you come from?' Satan answered the Lord, "From roaming through the earth and going back and forth on it." Then the Lord said to Satan, "Have you considered my servant Job? There is no one on earth like him; he is blameless and upright, a man who fears God and shuns evil." "Does Job fear God for nothing?" Satan replied. "Have you not put a hedge around him and his household and everything he has? You have blessed the work of his hands, so that his flocks and herds are spread throughout the land. But now stretch out your hand and strike everything he has, and he will surely curse you to your face." The Lord said to Satan, "Very well, then, everything he has is in your power, but on the man himself do not lay a finger." Then Satan went out from the <u>presence</u> of the Lord* (Job 1:6–12).

We have Lucifer in the presence of God. He and His angels conversed with Satan like they were friends.

God started talking about His servant Job with great pride. He explained how Job was righteous, blameless, and upright, and that no one was like him on earth. God knew full well that Lucifer's reaction would be jealousy and hate toward Job. God drew him out for a challenge that would alter the course of Job's life and the lives of his family.

Job became a pawn between two of the universe's greatest powers: God against Satan or good against evil. Job could do nothing about it. His destiny had been determined.

With God's permission granted, Lucifer attacked Job with tenacity. In Job 1:13–22, we find that he [Satan] first takes away his livelihood by attacking his livestock and killing his servants. Then he attacked his food supply and his transportation. He killed more of his servants, and finally he destroyed his home and killed his children.

In addition, with all that just happened, Job fell to the ground and worshipped the God who gave Lucifer permission to attack and kill and said, "Naked I came from my mother's womb, and naked I will depart. The Lord gave and the Lord has taken away; may the name of the Lord be praised."

In all of this, Job didn't charge God with wrongdoing, and he didn't sin. I don't think Job had any knowledge at that time that God had given Lucifer permission to cause all of this misery in his life. Scripture shows no reference to him knowing. I do believe, however, that if he would have known that God had allowed all of these things to happen, he might have had a different opinion about his God. With everything that occurred, you might think that poor Job had been through enough. Unfortunately for him, this was just the beginning of his misery.

> *On another day the angels came to present themselves before the Lord, and Satan also came with them to present himself before him. And the Lord said to Satan, "Where have you come from?" Satan answered the Lord, "From roaming throughout the earth, going back and forth on it." Then the Lord said to Satan, "Have you considered my servant Job? There is no one on earth like him; he is blameless and upright, a man who fears God and shuns evil. And he still maintains his integrity, though you incited me against him to ruin him without any reason." "Skin for skin!" Satan replied. "A man will give all he has for his own life. But now stretch out your hand and strike his flesh and bones, and he will surely curse you to your face." The Lord said to Satan, "Very well, then, he is in your hands; but you must spare his life." So Satan went out from the presence of the Lord and afflicted Job with painful sores from the soles of his feet to the crown of his head* (Job 2:1–7 NIV).

I don't know about you, but this story really angers me. Why would God let Lucifer incite Him against an innocent man who only wanted to live a good life and serve the God he loved? This almost sounds like what happened in the Garden of Eden when the serpent tempted Eve to eat from the tree of knowledge of good and evil. Instead, though, Lucifer had incited God against an innocent man to destroy him (Job 2:3).

This story solidifies the fact that the only power Lucifer has is the power that God gives him. Anytime evil is done, whether it's destruction, disease, pestilence, war, murder, or any form of evil, Lucifer has to and must get permission from God to proceed.

Now I know this is hard to swallow as a believer. In all of this tragedy that took place in Job's life with God's full permission and cooperation, a very strong message of hope and redemption can be found. Even though Job was blameless and upright, he was still human. God had to show through this man's life that no flesh can be saved without Him. The righteousness of man is filth in the eyes of God.

God had put a hedge of protection around Job and blessed him to prepare him for this test of his faith. He knew full well what the outcome would be. He was showing Lucifer and the world that throughout history when a man loves the Lord with all of his heart, mind, and soul, there are no obstacles he can't face.

If you read the full story, Job did get upset. He did question God as to why He had allowed these things to happen in his life. Still, he maintained his faith in God, and that is what brought him through this trial by fire. Through that test, he fell more in love with God. Everything that Job lost was restored seven times more than what he previously had.

Lucifer is God's tool to show the universe that sin and rebellion will not work. That's why God uses him for this purpose. He wants all of creation, good and evil, to know the power of love and mercy that's displayed through faith in Him.

We have to understand we were created for God's pleasure and will. He's controlling all things, which includes the destiny of everyone who has ever lived in the past, present, and future.

The future could be another hundred million years. Therefore, if God wants and decides that He's going to teach us for the next six thousand years about the way He wants the universe to run, who am I to question His sovereignty? Think about the size of the universe. Consider the trillions of planets that are out there in space over fifteen billion light-years away. Those are only what we know of at the writing of this book.

What if God was preparing his newest creation of humanity (His bride) to become like Him so that each of us will be governing our own planets? Remember back in Genesis 3:22: "And the LORD God said, 'The man has now become like one of us, knowing good and evil. He must not be allowed to reach out his hand and take also from the tree of life and eat, and live forever.'" (Take notice of these words: "The man has now become like *one of us*.")

Of course, this is speculation on my part, but it is a possibility that God is preparing man to help govern His universe under His sovereign lordship. One must remember one small book can't contain all of the knowledge of God and His intentions for humans in the distant future.

We'll experience what Lucifer never could comprehend, which is that loving God is about hope, which leads to obedience to Him. The time for man's reinstatement is soon at hand. God has created us to rule and reign with Him, to replace those who decided they would follow their own will instead of God's will.

Lucifer's rebellion changed the course of the universe, but God in His infinite wisdom knew beforehand what would be needed to restore all things back to His original intent. Jesus Christ would and did sacrifice His own life in order to guarantee man's restoration to his rightful place in God's universe.

Through His obedience to the Father, He secured our eternal salvation.

Author's Note

God in His abundant mercy is calling us back unto Himself, and we must return to the place of reverent submission and repentance. We must seek His face before the fire of judgment falls because, child of God, judgment first begins in the house of God.

Repent child of God. Repent and seek His face. Turn away from the path that leads to destruction. Fall on your face in reverent submission and cry out to God with a sincere heart to save our wretched souls from the destruction that is sure to come.

God has a history of putting His children through the fire to refine and purify them so that He can save them. God's Word says He is the same yesterday, today, and forever, so don't be duped into believing it can't happen to you.

I've been there, child of God. I have walked down the road of chastisement and correction. I have seen the power of God's mercy drive compromise and sin out of my own heart and life. Believe me, it is a terrible thing to fall into the hands of a living God, a God who loves you enough to strip you of every worldly thing. Every dream and hope will be put on hold for years until He removes your selfishness, anger, rebellion, bitterness, and rage so that you can claim what He laid down His life for: your eternal soul.

About the Author

Paul Schippel received his Bachelor of Arts in Biblical Studies in 1998, from Advanced Theological Seminary. He has also served as associate pastor for Faith in God Ministries in North Ft. Myers, Florida. He subsequently served as the outreach pastor and the adult teacher for Cape Coral Assembly of God, teaching Bible prophecy and personal growth.

In the summer of 2010, Paul received a visitation from the Holy Spirit that changed his life forever. He was given a bold Old Testament message for the New Testament Church. It was a message of hope through repentance on a corporate and personal level so that we can prepare for the return of Christ.

Schippel was born in Montgomery, West Virginia, but was raised in Florida. He left home at the age of fourteen to get away from physical and emotional abuse. At fifteen, he met Christ in a Pentecostal Church in Antioch, California. Because of the false-prosperity gospel and the deep-seated false religious teaching that became prevalent within the Church, he pursued a career in business that has lasted until this present day.

Schippel has four children and two grandchildren. He lives with his wife and family in Cape Coral, Florida.

www.ingramcontent.com/pod-product-compliance
Lightning Source LLC
Chambersburg PA
CBHW021436080526
44588CB00009B/551